HOMEMADE PASTA
made simple

homemade PASTA made simple

A Pasta Cookbook with Easy Recipes & Lessons
to Make Fresh Pasta Any Night

Manuela Zangara

ROCKRIDGE
PRESS

For general information on our other products and services or to obtain technical support, please contact our Customer Care Department within the United States at (866) 744-2665, or outside the United States at (510) 253-0500.

Rockridge Press publishes its books in a variety of electronic and print formats. Some content that appears in print may not be available in electronic books, and vice versa.

TRADEMARKS: Rockridge Press and the Rockridge Press logo are trademarks or registered trademarks of Callisto Media, Inc., and/or its affiliates, in the United States and other countries, and may not be used without written permission. All other trademarks are the property of their respective owners. Rockridge Press is not associated with any product or vendor mentioned in this book.

Photography © Paul S. Bartholomew/Offset, cover; The Picture Pantry/Stockfood, pp. ii & 108; Kema Food Culture/Stocksy, pp. vi, xi (right), 218 & back cover; Ina Peters/Stocksy, p. xi (left); Pierre Hussenot/PhotoCuisine/Stockfood, p. xi (middle); Rua Castilho/Stockfood, pp. 2 & 76; Hendey, Magdalena Hendey/Stockfood, p. 10; Snowflake Studios Inc./Stockfood, p. 20; Tom Swalens/PhotoCuisine/Stockfood, p. 44; Thorsten kleine Holthaus/Stockfood, p. 148; Erin Brooks/Stockfood, p, 172; Kues/Shutterstock.com, p. 172 (background).

Illustrations © Tom Bingham 2017

ISBN: Print 978-1-62315-918-4 | eBook 978-1-62315-919-1

To Clint, Victoria, and Georgia for always believing in me.
Your support and unconditional love are my strength.
Thank you for being my taste testers and guinea pigs—
I am glad you never tire of pasta!

CONTENTS

sauces

G ROWING UP, I REMEMBER eagerly awaiting the weekend, when my parents and I would often make pasta at home. In the kitchen of our apartment in Milan, we would make lasagna sheets, pappardelle, tortellini, and all sorts of different pasta. And while we were working on the pasta, a pot full of pasta sauce would always be simmering away on the stove, filling the whole house with its delicious aroma.

Even now that I am a grown-up, I still associate pasta making with family time and a pervasive sense of comfort. Preparing pasta from scratch—turning flour, eggs, and water into something beautiful and different every time—is an act of love. It requires passion, time, and a little effort, but it is not at all difficult. On the contrary, it can be incredibly easy and even relaxing. In fact, it is something that can be turned into a family ritual, an activity to share with the kids and get them involved in the process. I am sure they will have lots of fun getting their hands dirty with flour and manipulating pieces of dough, just like I used to as a child in Milan.

Italians have been making pasta at home for ages. Pasta being a poor man's dish, people would often use whatever ingredients they had available and whatever was cheapest. The best part is that many of the recipes have been passed down from one generation to the next and are deeply rooted in the local areas. This is why there are so many regional variations of shapes, ingredients, and stuffing. Something as simple as ravioli can be completely different in Friuli than in Sardinia.

I know that nowadays ready-made pasta is easily available, but like all things, the satisfaction of eating something made from scratch makes your own fresh pasta taste better. After all, your love and care is in there, right? Besides, you don't need to rely on the shapes the store has in stock: They don't have orecchiette? No drama, we can make some in just a few steps and with just two ingredients! Wait, what? It's true. You need only two ingredients!

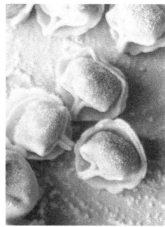

People who have little or no experience in making pasta at home often ask me how to do it. What are the techniques they should learn? The task seems so overwhelming that they don't know how to begin. This book makes the process less intimidating through introductory lessons and tutorials that help you truly understand how pasta is made. It's been designed for beginners, with the attention to detail and clarity you need to master the basic skills of pasta making and start whipping up your own fresh pasta every night of the week.

In this step-by-step guide to the craft of homemade pasta, I will gradually lead you through all pasta-making techniques, from the easier ones to those that will require you to put into practice the skills you have developed. I will also go through the equipment and ingredients needed, and you will be surprised to learn that you don't require anything fancy to start creating your pasta shapes. I am also ready to bet that you already have all the ingredients you require in your pantry. No need to go out and buy expensive stuff from the store. You will also be provided with foolproof basic pasta dough recipes that are so easy to make, you will be able to memorize and master them in no time!

The recipe chapters are divided by type of pasta—hand-shaped pasta, ribbon-cut pasta, stuffed pasta, and gnocchi and *gnudi*—with a final chapter offering fabulous sauce recipes that will give you the freedom to mix and match as you please. By the end of the book, you will be making pasta like a pro!

Discover how easy (and fun!) it is to make pasta from scratch. Don't be intimidated: Making pasta at home is as simple as eating it!

getting started

W E WILL BEGIN BY TAKING STOCK of the basic ingredients and equipment you need. You may be surprised to realize that you already have all of the necessary ingredients in your kitchen and that you don't need any special tools to make pasta at home.

After that, I will share with you my know-by-heart pasta dough recipes—the only ones you will ever need—to make perfect pasta in your kitchen.

Last, we will go through all the techniques that you will need to start making your own fresh pasta. Valuable tutorials will set you on the path to success.

chapter 1
INGREDIENTS & EQUIPMENT

I KNOW THIS ALL SOUNDS PRETTY EXCITING, and I am sure you can't wait to try making your own pasta. However, before you get your hands covered in flour and eggs, let's take a closer look at what you'll need and why. That way, you'll be all set for success.

the ingredients

Making pasta is easy—I always say it's easier than baking a cake—but it can be intimidating when you are just starting out. I've got some good news for you: All homemade pasta is made from just a handful of common ingredients that you probably already have in your kitchen. Let's see what they are.

FLOUR

Pasta can be made with different types of flour. In fact, we use a variety of grains to give our pasta specific flavors or colors. However, wheat is the most common grain when it comes to homemade pasta.

Easy, right? Well, sort of, as not all wheat is the same. In Italy, we mainly use two different types of wheat: common wheat and durum wheat.

Common wheat is perfect for making bread, but it doesn't have as much gluten as durum wheat. A flour made from common wheat is weak, and the dough made from it tends to break easily and become slippery when cooked. That is why pasta made with common wheat flour requires eggs, which provide protein that acts a bit like gluten when it comes to dough making. All-purpose and 00 (spoken aloud as "zero-zero") flours are both made from common wheat, and they both work perfectly well for egg-based pasta.

Pasta made using 00 or all-purpose flour and eggs is usually smooth and silky. This kind of pasta is traditionally found in the North of Italy, where common wheat has always been a staple crop and readily available. Most stuffed pasta and ribbon pasta are made with all-purpose or 00 flour because these flours make dough that is pliable and easy to roll.

Durum wheat is a very hard, yellow-colored wheat with a high protein content, especially gluten. This makes it easier to transform it into pasta shapes without having to add eggs.

Pasta made from durum wheat flour has more bite to it, and it tends to remain *al dente*, an Italian phrase meaning literally, "to the tooth"—it's a shorthand for the proper cooked pasta texture, which should be somewhat firm. This kind of pasta is more common in Southern Italy, an area that is famous throughout the world for its durum wheat. Almost all hand-shaped pasta is made from durum wheat, as the dough made from it is stiffer and therefore more suitable for hand shaping.

A word of advice: Do not confuse durum wheat flour with semolina flour. They both come from the same kind of hard wheat, but semolina flour is much coarser than durum wheat flour and is not used to make pasta. We use semolina flour in other recipes, including Gnocchi alla Romana (page 166), a traditional recipe from Rome.

EGGS

When making egg-based pasta, eggs play a fundamental role in your success rate.

- Use only fresh eggs, of the highest possible quality.

- Break the eggs into a separate bowl before adding them to the flour to make sure they are not spoiled.

- For best results, bring the eggs to room temperature before using them in your dough.

- When making egg pasta dough, always use large eggs with an average weight of about 2 ounces each.

WATER

When making durum wheat-based pasta, always use lukewarm water. This will make kneading the dough much easier, and the dough will become more pliable.

EXTRA-VIRGIN OLIVE OIL

Even though it is not necessary, extra-virgin olive oil can be added to both egg-based pasta dough and durum wheat-based pasta dough. Oil makes the dough a little bit more elastic.

Traditionally it is not required and I do not usually add any. However, if you want to use it, choose a light and fruity extra-virgin olive oil so the flavor doesn't overpower the final taste of your pasta. Do not use more than 1 to 2 tablespoons when making pasta for four people.

SEA SALT

Adding salt to pasta dough is not at all required. In fact, the tiny grains of salt could make rolling the dough a bit harder. Pasta absorbs salt when you cook it, so it is more important to add salt to the cooking water than to the dough itself. If you absolutely want to add salt to the dough, use the finest salt you can find and don't add more than 1 teaspoon when making pasta for four people. Italians usually use sea salt for cooking, so I've specified sea salt for use in the recipes that call for it. You can use it to season your pasta cooking water, too.

the equipment

Now that you know what ingredients you will require, let's have a look at the tools that you will need to prepare the recipes in this book. There is a variety of equipment that will help you create beautifully shaped pasta—some of these tools are essential, while others are needed only for specialty pasta. You will be pleased to learn that you already own the majority of the items on this list. I have described the essential pieces first and have included a few more specialized items, in case you are interested. Please keep in mind that while some of these tools could make your life easier, the majority of the pasta shapes described in this book can be made simply by using your hands, a rolling pin, and/or a knife.

ESSENTIAL TOOLS

These are the tools that you really can't make pasta without. But don't panic! Most of these are items you already own.

Baking sheets: You need three baking sheets (10 by 15 inches in size) on which to place your ready pasta before cooking it. Make sure to always dust the baking sheets with a couple of tablespoons of flour so that the pasta doesn't stick to the surface.

Big wooden board or big cutting board: You need a big wooden board—or at least a big wooden cutting board—to give pasta like orecchiette and *strascinati* their characteristic rough surface to which the sauce clings.

Cookie/pasta cutters: Cookie cutters can be very useful when making stuffed pasta. You need a heart-shaped cookie cutter to make *cuori* and a star-shaped cookie cutter to make *stelle*. You also need round pasta/cookie cutters to make different shapes of stuffed pasta. You will need one each of 1½-inch, 2½-inch, 3-inch, and 5-inch diameters. Alternatively, you can use a glass or a bowl of the same diameter as a guide and a nonserrated knife to cut around it.

Crinkle-edge pastry wheel and/or pizza cutter: You need a crinkle-edge pastry wheel to make stuffed pasta, like ravioli or *caramelle*, look prettier, and you also need it to give ribbon pasta, like *mafalde* and *rombi*, its characteristic shape. In some cases, a pizza cutter can be used instead of a crinkle-edge pastry wheel or a knife. You can cut out more pasta in less time if you use one.

Knitting needle: You need a knitting needle—size 0 or 1—to make pasta like *maccheroni al ferretto, fusilli avellinesi,* or *busiati.*

Knives: You need a good, sharp, nonserrated cutting knife to cut out your dough and turn it into pasta or gnocchi. You'll use a round-edged table knife to give pasta like orecchiette and *cozzette* its typical shape.

Metal cake spatula: You need a round-edged metal cake spatula to give pasta like *strascinati* its typical shape. It serves the same purpose as a table knife, but it is much bigger and better suited for broader shapes of pasta. You can use it instead of the specific tool to make strascinati, which is very hard to find.

Pasta machine: This is a very useful piece of equipment to have, especially if you are planning to make pasta often or for more than two people. It saves you a lot of time and effort, as it does the rolling for you, and it also ensures a uniform thickness to the pasta sheets. You can get a manual machine or a motorized one. I have a manual one and I love it, but the choice is yours. Pasta machines often come with attachments to cut pasta ribbons, like *tagliatelle* and/or *tagliolini*, which are very useful too.

Plastic wrap: Plastic wrap is essential to keep your dough from drying out. Make sure to always wrap the dough tightly with plastic wrap before leaving it to rest. You should also use it to cover the dough whenever you are not working on it. If the dough dries out, it will create a crust and start breaking, and it will not be possible to shape it anymore.

Potato ricer: A potato ricer is very useful for making gnocchi. It processes the potatoes (and other vegetables) by forcing them through a sheet of small holes, giving a smoother texture to the mash, which in turn gives you much smoother and more uniform gnocchi dough.

Rolling pin: A long, thin, European-style rolling pin is useful when making pasta that requires rolling out, like ribbon pasta, for example. It is essential if you do not have a pasta machine.

Kitchen scale: Making pasta from scratch is very easy when you have the right dough, and to obtain the right dough, the best thing to do is to precisely weigh the ingredients. This is particularly important when you are just starting out and are not yet familiar with the correct look and feel of a good pasta. A weighing scale is a really important tool when it comes to pasta making, and I highly recommend you use one.

NONESSENTIAL TOOLS

The following tools are nice to have and come in handy for making specialty pasta shapes, but they are by no means necessary.

Big bowl: You may use a bowl to bring together all your dough ingredients before transferring it onto your work surface to knead it.

Chitarra: A *chitarra* is a "pasta guitar" made up of a wooden frame strung with music wire, which is used to cut fresh pasta into strands. You can make Spaghetti alla Chitarra (page 106) with it, and it is a common pasta-making tool in Southern Italy.

Dough scraper: A dough scraper is a tool used to manipulate dough and to clean the surfaces on which the dough has been worked. It is generally a small sheet of stainless steel (approximately 3 by 5 inches) with a handle of wood or plastic. It can be very useful when making pasta dough, but it's not essential.

Gnocchi board: A gnocchi board is a small wooden board with ridges that give gnocchi their traditional shape. If you can find it, the one that comes with the mini rolling pin is also perfect for making *garganelli*. This tool is inexpensive and a great gadget to have, but it is not essential. If you don't have one, you can use a fork to give gnocchi their typical ridges.

Food processor: If you have a food processor, you can use it to blend all the ingredients to bring the dough together until the flour looks like coarse breadcrumbs. Then you can transfer the mixture onto the work surface and knead it.

Pasta frame and drying rack: A pasta frame is a wooden frame fitted with a thin mesh. It's used to keep short pasta to dry. A drying rack is used to hang long pasta to dry.

Stand mixer: If you have a stand mixer, you can use it to make your dough. You will need both paddle and hook attachments to bring the dough together and knead it.

chapter 2

THE DOUGH

Now that you are familiar with the ingredients and the tools required to make your own pasta at home, let's focus on the next subject: the dough. In this chapter I will guide you through the steps required to create perfect dough. I will share some of the secrets I've learned through 25 years of making my own pasta, and I will share my foolproof dough recipes. The recipes include Know-by-Heart Egg Pasta Dough (page 14), Know-by-Heart Durum Wheat Pasta Dough (page 16), and Gluten-Free Pasta Dough (page 17). You will also find some interesting tips on how to color and flavor your pasta dough in different ways. Rest assured, making the perfect pasta dough from scratch is easier than it seems, and with my step-by-step directions, you will turn into a professional pasta maker in no time. Put on your apron and let's get started!

making pasta dough

While making pasta dough by hand is very easy, there are a few important practices to remember. Once you have mastered the technique explained below, it will become second nature to you, and the whole process will become very easy. You see, you will be making pasta like a pro in no time. After all, there are only four easy steps to follow to obtain the perfect pasta dough. Let's go through them in detail.

MAKE A WELL

Weigh the flour and pour it onto your work surface in a pile. Make a hole in the center of the pile using your fingertips. This is called a *well*. The well has to be big enough to fit the eggs. Break your eggs one at a time into a separate bowl to make sure they are fresh, and then add them to the well. Beat the eggs with a fork until smooth. If you are using any other ingredients—salt, extra-virgin olive oil, and/or ingredients to color the dough—this is the time to add them.

MIX THE INGREDIENTS

Using the tips of your fingers, gradually start pushing the flour into the beaten eggs, incorporating it a little at a time, until everything is well combined. When the dough is still wet and sticky, but holding together, scrape off any dough sticking to your hands and to the work surface. Start to fold additional flour into the dough with your hands, rotating the dough by a quarter each time, to incorporate the flour more evenly.

KNEAD

Once the dough feels firm and dry, and comes together into a ball, it's time to start kneading. To knead, simply press the heel of your hand into the ball of dough, pushing forward and down. Rotate the ball and do it again. Knead the dough for 5 to 10 minutes, or until it becomes very smooth and elastic. If your dough feels wet, add more flour as necessary. Kneading the dough well is really important to develop the gluten necessary to get the perfect pasta texture. Do not knead the dough for more than 10 minutes, since the gluten will have already developed by then and you will end up overkneading the dough, which will make it tough and difficult to roll, and the resulting pasta will be very chewy.

BOWL OR WELL?
If you are just starting out experimenting with pasta dough making, I suggest you start mixing your ingredients in a bowl. This will prevent the flour from spreading everywhere, and you will have less to clean up at the end. When the dough comes together, transfer it to the work surface and knead.

HOW LONG TO KNEAD?
An underkneaded dough will not have the same kind of spring as a properly kneaded dough. Kneading the dough for at least 5 minutes is important to develop the gluten necessary to make perfect pasta. Don't knead the dough for more than 10 minutes, since the gluten will have already developed by then, and overkneading the dough will make it tough.

USE A DOUGH SCRAPER:
Use a dough scraper instead of a knife to scrape off the dough from the work surface while making the dough. It is much more efficient.

LET THE DOUGH REST

Once you have your ball of kneaded dough, wrap it tightly in plastic wrap and let it rest for 30 minutes. Resting your dough is very important. When you knead it, you help develop the gluten in the flour. Gluten makes your dough springy and elastic. If you try to roll the dough immediately after kneading it, you'll find it to be very difficult, as the dough will simply spring back on itself. The resting time allows the flour to continue to hydrate, and the gluten network to relax, thus making the rolling step much easier.

The technique for making durum wheat pasta dough is exactly the same as the one described for egg pasta dough. Simply substitute lukewarm water for the eggs.

know-by-heart egg pasta dough

I know there are many pasta dough recipes that claim to be easy, yet when you read through them, they are anything but simple and often include a puzzlingly long list of ingredients. The truth is, to make good, traditional egg pasta, you need only two ingredients: flour and eggs. Sure, you can add some light-flavored extra-virgin olive oil and/or salt if you like, but Italians seldom do. The proportion is 3½ ounces of flour and 1 large egg per person. If you keep that in mind, you can easily memorize this recipe and make it for any number of people you like. Now, that is easy, right? This two-ingredient egg pasta dough works very well for stuffed pasta, ribbon pasta, and even some hand-shaped pasta, like farfalle and garganelli, making it the best and most versatile pasta dough recipe ever. SERVES 4

PREP TIME: 45 MINUTES, RESTING TIME INCLUDED

14 ounces 00 flour or all-purpose flour

4 large eggs (weighing about 2 ounces each)

1. Weigh the flour and mound it on a board or in a bowl. Make a well in the center of the mound. Crack the eggs in a separate bowl and pour them into the well.

2. Beat the eggs with a fork until smooth. Using the tips of your fingers, mix the eggs with the flour, incorporating it a little at a time, until everything is combined.

3. Knead the dough for 5 to 10 minutes, or until the dough is smooth. Make the dough into a ball, wrap it in plastic wrap to prevent it from drying out, and let it rest for 30 minutes before rolling it out and turning it into pasta.

In a Food Processor

You can make your pasta dough in a food processor. To do so, simply put all the ingredients in the bowl of your food processor and blend for a few seconds, or until the flour looks like coarse breadcrumbs.

Transfer the mixture onto a floured work surface and knead it for 5 to 10 minutes, or until the dough is smooth. This will develop the gluten you need to obtain the perfect pasta texture.

Then make the dough into a ball. Wrap it in plastic wrap to prevent it from drying out, and let it rest for 30 minutes before rolling it out and turning it into pasta.

This method applies to all the pasta dough recipes in this book.

In a Stand Mixer

You can also make your pasta dough in a stand mixer. To do so, fit your stand mixer with the paddle attachment, put all the ingredients in the bowl, and mix on low speed until the ingredients come together.

Swap the paddle attachment with the hook attachment and knead on medium-high speed for 5 minutes, or until the dough is smooth. This will develop the gluten you need to obtain the perfect pasta texture.

Make the dough into a ball, wrap it in plastic wrap to prevent it from drying out, and let it rest for 30 minutes before rolling it out and turning it into pasta.

This method applies to all the pasta dough recipes in this book.

know-by-heart durum wheat pasta dough

Making durum wheat pasta dough is just as easy as making egg pasta dough, if not easier. The technique is exactly the same, and so is the number of ingredients required, but in this case you simply need durum wheat flour and water. The only trick here is to use lukewarm water, which will make kneading the dough a lot easier. The proportion is 3½ ounces of durum wheat flour and 1¾ ounces of water per person. If you keep this in mind, you can use this recipe to make pasta for any number of people you like. Not hard at all, is it? And the best part is that this recipe yields the perfect durum wheat pasta dough. It works very well for all kinds of hand-shaped pasta. It even works for some stuffed pasta, like *culurgiones*, and ribbon pasta, like *lagane*, *mafalde*, *sagne*, *spaghetti alla chitarra*, and *stringozzi*. Durum wheat pasta dough is also a great vegan option, as it contains no eggs. **SERVES 4**

PREP TIME: 45 MINUTES, RESTING TIME INCLUDED

14 ounces durum wheat flour

¾ cup lukewarm water (about 7 ounces), plus up to 3 tablespoons if needed

1. Weigh the flour and mound it on a board or in a bowl. Make a well in the center and add ¾ cup of lukewarm water to it.

2. Using the tips of your fingers, mix the water with the flour, incorporating it a little at a time, until everything is combined. Add the remaining 3 tablespoons of water, a little at a time, if required.

3. Knead the dough for 5 to 10 minutes, or until the dough is smooth. Make into a ball, wrap it in plastic wrap to prevent it from drying out, and let it rest for 30 minutes before turning it into pasta.

gluten-free pasta dough

The key to making the perfect gluten-free pasta dough is to use a mix of different flours. I have experimented with many, but in the end, I found out that mixing rice flour, potato starch, and cornstarch gives the best results. Do not confuse cornstarch with cornmeal, which is yellow and much coarser than the powdery white cornstarch you need for this recipe. As you still need to make the dough elastic to be able to have good-quality pasta that doesn't break and become slippery when cooked, you need to add eggs to it. Eggs bind like gluten when it comes to dough making. You also require more wet ingredients since gluten-free flours tend to absorb more liquids than flours with gluten. That being the case, this recipe has a longer ingredient list, but the technique is just as easy as the one for the other types of pasta dough. Please be advised this dough works best for pasta ribbons and stuffed pasta. You can use it for hand-shaped pasta, too, but it will take a little longer to cook. Always taste your pasta before draining it to make sure it's cooked through. SERVES 4

PREP TIME: 45 MINUTES, RESTING TIME INCLUDED

5 ounces gluten-free rice flour, plus more if required

2 ounces potato starch

1 tablespoon cornstarch

2 tablespoons xanthan gum

1 tablespoon extra-virgin olive oil

3 large eggs (weighing about 2 ounces each)

1. Weigh the rice flour and potato starch, and combine them with the cornstarch and xanthan gum on a board or in a bowl. Make a well in the center. Crack the eggs in a separate bowl and pour them into the well together with the olive oil.

2. Beat the eggs and oil with a fork until smooth. Using the tips of your fingers, mix the eggs with the flour, incorporating it a little at a time, until everything is combined.

3. Knead the dough, adding a little extra rice flour if required, for 5 to 10 minutes or until the dough is smooth. Make into a ball.

4. Wrap the ball in plastic wrap to prevent it from drying out, and let it rest for 30 minutes before rolling it out and turning it into pasta.

Flavoring and Coloring Pasta Dough

When you are confident enough with the basic recipes, you can experiment with flavoring and coloring your pasta dough. As you may need to make a few adjustments to the quantity of flour you use, I suggest you try these recipes only after you know what the correct dough feels like. There are no exact measures, as it all depends on how wet the coloring ingredient is.

There are many ways you can add color to your basic dough. Below are a few ideas to get you started.

GREEN: You can make green pasta by adding 1½ ounces of wilted spinach for every 14 ounces of flour to your basic pasta dough. Make sure to squeeze out all the water from your spinach, cut it very finely with a knife, and mix it with the flour well when making the dough. You may need a little extra flour, depending on how wet the spinach is. Then proceed as if you were making regular dough.

YELLOW: You can make yellow pasta by adding 1 teaspoon of saffron powder for every 14 ounces of flour to your basic pasta dough. Mix the saffron with the flour and proceed as if you were making regular dough.

RED: You can make red pasta by adding 4 tablespoons of tomato paste for every 14 ounces of flour to your basic pasta dough. Mix the tomato paste with the flour and eggs or water, then proceed as if you were making regular dough.

For a more uniformly colored dough, make it in a food processor. Blending the ingredients together will help spread the color evenly.

chapter 3

THE SKILLS

I N THIS CHAPTER, I WILL GUIDE YOU through a series of techniques with easy tutorials designed to introduce you to some important basic homemade pasta skills. Since we all learn by doing, you will also find a lesson with every technique, so that you can put what you just learned into practice. While you can always jump straight into the recipes if you'd like, the lessons in this chapter are designed to be the perfect entry point for pasta making. I will share some tips and tricks on how to make pasta in a faster and easier way, and will shed some light on a few misconceptions. By the end of the chapter, and with a little bit of practice, I assure you that you will master essential skills, like rolling, shaping, cutting, stuffing, and drying, and you will be ready to start cooking perfectly made pasta.

rolling pasta dough

Rolling pasta dough using a pasta machine is very simple. This technique can be used on all the dough recipes in this book and not exclusively on egg pasta dough, as you might have thought. You will need this technique to make all ribbon-cut pasta, stuffed pasta, and some hand-shaped pasta, too. You'll be using this skill often, so it is an important one to learn.

How thin you need to roll the dough depends on the specific shape you want to make. You will find this information listed under each pasta recipe published in the next chapters. Keep in mind that the majority of pasta machines available on the market have settings that go between #1, which gives you the thickest sheet of pasta, and #9, which gives you an almost transparent sheet of pasta. Follow the below steps to get smooth and silky pasta sheets that are perfect to be transformed into all sorts of delicious pasta shapes.

1. After your pasta dough has rested for 30 minutes, you are ready to start rolling it into sheets.

2. Remove the dough from the plastic wrap. With a sharp knife, cut off a piece of pasta dough (about an eighth of the whole) and rewrap the remaining dough, to prevent it from drying out while you are not working with it.

3. Using your hands, flatten the piece you have cut out into a rectangular shape.

FIGURE 3.1

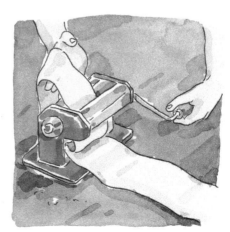

FIGURE 3.2

FLOUR
Remember to dust your pasta sheet and your work surface with a little flour before feeding the dough through the machine. Be careful not to add too much flour, or your pasta dough will become too dry and start to break.

IDEAL THICKNESS
Even though each shape has its own thickness, the majority of pasta will require you to roll the dough between settings #7 and #8. As a rule of thumb, stuffed pasta will require a thinner pasta sheet than ribbon and hand-shaped pasta.

MOTOR OR MANUAL?
Nowadays, pasta machines come with their own motor to save you time and effort. It is helpful to have a motorized pasta machine, but not at all essential.

4. Turn the dial of the pasta machine to the thickest setting (#1). Dust the dough rectangle with a little flour. Starting with one of the narrower sides of the rectangle, feed it through the rollers.

5. Fold one side of the sheet of dough over the middle, and fold the other side over that to form three layers.

6. Starting with one of the narrower ends of the folded dough, feed the pasta through the pasta machine, again at the thickest setting (Figure 3.1). Repeat this folding and rolling technique on the thickest setting at least a couple of times, or until the dough is an even thickness. This will help make the pasta smooth and silky.

7. Now you can start rolling the sheet thinner, by turning the dial to the next setting (#2).

8. Roll the pasta sheet through the machine repeatedly, adjusting the setting each time, until your reach the desired thinness (Figure 3.2). You don't need to fold the dough between settings after setting #1.

9. Trim the edges with a sharp knife, if necessary, to make them straight.

lasagna sheets

The lasagna sheet is the simplest handmade pasta shape that requires you to put the technique of rolling pasta dough to use. All you have to do is roll the pasta dough until the required thickness is achieved and cut it with a sharp, nonserrated knife into rectangular pieces. It is usually the first type of pasta that Italians learn how to make from scratch. You can use these pasta sheets for Lasagna Sheets (page 78) and Cannelloni (see note on page 79), but they are also the base for many other ribbon pasta types, like Quadrucci (page 94), Rombi (page 96), and Maltagliati (page 80). This is why learning how to make lasagna sheets properly will bring you a huge step closer to becoming a pasta-making expert. All you need is just a little practice.

00 or all-purpose flour, for dusting

1 batch Know-by-Heart Egg Pasta Dough (page 14)

1. Dust three baking sheets with 00 or all-purpose flour.

2. Roll the dough (see page 22) and feed the prepared egg pasta sheet through the machine, adjusting the settings, until setting #7. If the sheet of pasta gets too long, cut it in half with a knife.

3. You can do this with a rolling pin, too. Make the dough as thin and uniform as possible.

4. Using a sharp, nonserrated knife, cut into 6-by-4-inch sheets.

5. Transfer to the prepared baking sheets.

6. Repeat the above steps until all of the dough has been rolled and cut.

hand-shaping pasta

Shaping pasta using your hands is possibly the most fun cooking experience ever. Trust me, you will love it.

To be precise, it would be more correct to talk about multiple hand-shaping techniques and traditions rather than just one single technique. Since pasta making is very much linked to local cuisines, you can easily imagine that each area (or even town!) in Italy has its own traditional pasta shape, and with each pasta shape comes a different technique. As the majority of hand-shaped pasta is made with durum wheat dough, it is easy to understand how this kind of pasta is much more commonly found in the South of Italy, an area famous for its durum wheat. Compared to egg-based dough, durum wheat dough is much better suited to hand-shaped pasta, since the dough is firmer and easier to work by hand without having to roll it out first. There are, however, a few exceptions to this rule, as some hand-shaped pastas—like Farfalle (page 52) or Garganelli (page 74), for example—are made with egg-based dough, rolled out first, and shaped by hand only later.

Most pasta shapes are made by rolling out ropes of dough with your fingertips. In some cases, these ropes of dough are then cut into different-sized pieces. How these pieces of dough are then turned into different shapes of pasta varies from region to region. I will guide you through each technique in more detail with each pasta shape recipe; however, below is a reasonably comprehensive list of hand-shaping techniques.

USING A KNIFE

In Apulia, an area famous both for its durum wheat and for its homemade pasta tradition, Orecchiette (page 72) are made by pressing down the pieces of dough with a round-edged kitchen knife on a wooden surface and then unfurling them over the thumb in the opposite direction to form a concave shape. Strascinati (page 60) and Cozzette (page 58) are made in a very similar way but differ in size and in the fact that they don't get unfurled over the thumb after being shaped with the knife.

USING YOUR FINGERS

In Campania, and again in certain areas of Apulia, Cavatelli (page 46), Cavatellini (page 48), and Cicatelli (page 50) are made by pressing down the cut pieces of rope with the fingers of one hand. They differ only in size, cavatellini being the shortest, made using only the index finger, and cicatelli being the longest, made using three fingers.

USING A KNITTING NEEDLE

Other pasta typical of the South of Italy is made by rolling the ropes of dough around a knitting needle: Fusilli Avellinesi (page 68) from Campania, Busiati (page 70) from Sicily, and Maccheroni col Ferretto (page 66) are all pasta shapes that use this technique.

USING A GNOCCHI BOARD OR A FORK

On the island of Sardinia, Malloreddus (page 56) are made by pressing the pieces of rope on a gnocchi board or the tines of a fork with the thumb to give the pasta its characteristic ridged shape.

USING THE PALM OF YOUR HAND

Pastas like Pici (page 54) from Tuscany are made by simply rolling the ropes thinner and thinner with the palms of your hands. Strozzapreti (page 64) from Emilia-Romagna are made by first rolling and cutting the dough like broad Pappardelle (page 88). These are then rolled and twirled between the palms of your hands and broken into 3½-inch-long pieces.

USING THE SIDE OF YOUR HAND

Trofie (page 62), a traditional pasta shape from Liguria, are made by simply pinching out a small amount of dough and rolling it first with the palm of your hand into a thin rope. These small ropes are then twirled by rolling them at an angle with the side of your hand.

FAMILY AND FRIENDS
Shaping pasta by hand is a lot of fun, but it can be tiring, and if you are making a lot of pasta, it can also be quite time-consuming. Turn it into a shared activity to make with family and/or friends to finish faster.

KEEP IT COVERED
Just as for your egg pasta dough, keep your durum wheat dough covered at all times when you are not using it. If it dries out, you will not be able to shape your pasta properly.

FLOUR
Only lightly dust your work surface with flour, or your dough will become too slippery and you will not be able to roll your pasta into ropes and then shape it.

ROLLING THE DOUGH

There are two exceptions to the above methods. Farfalle (page 52) and Garganelli (page 74) are both made with egg pasta dough instead of durum wheat dough. As such, they both need to be rolled out into thin sheets of pasta before being given their traditional shapes by hand. Farfalle are made by simply cutting out small squares of thin pasta dough and pinching them in the middle to form "bow ties." Garganelli require you to roll the thin squares of dough around the handle of a wooden spoon and then roll them on a gnocchi board to give them their characteristic shape.

So, as you can see, in some cases all you need are your hands to turn a simple piece of dough into beautifully shaped pasta!

cavatelli

One of the easiest shapes to make is cavatelli. It is a short pasta with a shell-like appearance that curves inward a bit. Cavatelli are traditionally made in the Southern regions of Campania, Molise, Apulia, and Basilicata, where they are served with mussels and beans or meat-based sauces. While making cavatelli, you will be able to practice many of the hand-shaping pasta techniques covered in this chapter. First, you will roll out ropes of dough with your fingertips as if you were making gnocchi. Then you will cut the ropes into smaller pieces and shape cavatelli by pressing down the cut pieces of rope with the fingers of one hand. The more pressure you apply, the thinner the cavatelli will be. Try to keep the pressure uniform, or the cavatelli will not all cook at the same time and you may end up with a mix of hard and overcooked pasta on your plate. You do not need any special equipment to make this pasta shape, just a knife and your hands. Once you are confident at making cavatelli, you will be ready to make more challenging hand-shaped pasta.

Durum wheat flour, for dusting

1 batch Know-by-Heart Durum Wheat Pasta Dough (page 16)

1. Dust three baking sheets with durum wheat flour.

2. Take 3-inch balls of dough and roll them into ⅔-inch-thick ropes using your fingertips (Figure 3.3).

3. Cut these ropes into 1-inch-long pieces (Figure 3.4).

4. Put your index and middle fingers together and press them down on each piece of dough (Figure 3.5), rolling it toward you with a quick movement to create the desired shape (Figure 3.6).

5. Put the shaped pasta on the prepared baking sheets.

6. Repeat the above steps until you have used up all of the dough.

FIGURE 3.3

FIGURE 3.4

FIGURE 3.5

FIGURE 3.6

cutting ribbons

Pasta ribbons are flat strands of pasta, like Tagliatelle (page 92) or Fettuccine (page 90). Depending on the specific shape, ribbons can vary in length, thickness, and above all, width. Ribbon pasta can have straight or wavy edges, and many varieties can be easily made at home.

Now that you are an expert at rolling pasta and making lasagna sheets, making pasta ribbons will not be hard at all. This technique can be used for both egg pasta dough and durum wheat pasta dough, and it is used throughout Italy.

Nowadays, many pasta machines come with attachments for cutting ribbons, so you also have that option. You simply have to feed your rolled sheet of dough through the attachment to get your pasta ribbons. However, knowing how to cut pasta ribbons by hand gives you the flexibility to make more shapes and experiment with different recipes and widths.

Let me guide you through the few essential steps required to obtain perfectly hand-cut ribbons of pasta.

ROLLING

Make sure to roll the pasta as thin as the recipe requires. The majority of ribbon pasta is quite thin, usually setting #7 of the pasta machine, but there are some exceptions to this rule. Stringozzi (page 104), for example, are much thicker.

CUTTING

Once you have rolled the dough into the required thickness, you can cut the ribbons. To do this, dust the sheet of pasta with a little flour and let it rest for 5 minutes. Starting with one of the short sides, roll the sheet up like paper towels on a roll. Using a sharp, nonserrated knife, cut the pasta into slices of the required width.

UNFOLDING

Delicately open up the sliced pasta with your hands, dust with a little flour, and make it into a loose nest. Transfer to a baking sheet dusted with flour.

It is as easy as that. You will have enough pasta to serve the whole family in no time at all.

ROLLING BY HAND
If rolling the dough by hand, you will get a much bigger sheet of dough. It may be easier to divide the dough into smaller pieces and work on them separately until you are more confident with the hand-rolling technique.

FLOUR
Make sure you always dust the thin sheet of dough with flour before you roll it. If you don't, the pasta may stick to itself and you will not be able to use it. You will have to refeed it through the pasta machine and start again.

RESTING
Let the thin sheet of dough rest, uncovered, for 5 minutes before rolling and cutting it. This will make cutting easier and more precise. However, do not let it rest for more than 5 minutes, or it will dry out and the pasta will break.

No Pasta Machine, No Problem: Hand-Stretched Pasta Dough Tutorial

Having a pasta machine is great and it can save you a lot of time, but Italians have rolled dough by hand for centuries! So don't panic; with some practice, you can do it, too.

Divide the dough into quarters. Roll out one quarter at a time, keeping the rest of the dough wrapped in plastic wrap to prevent it from drying out. Very lightly dust your work surface with a little flour—not too much or your dough will slip when you try to roll it. A couple of teaspoons should be enough.

Shape the dough into a ball. Roll it out into a circle by stretching as well as pressing down. Stretch the dough by rolling a quarter way back onto the rolling pin and gently pushing the rolling pin away from you, while holding the rest of the dough. Turn the circle a quarter turn and repeat. Do this twice more.

Keep rolling and stretching the dough until the pasta is very thin and as uniform as possible.

Repeat with the remaining dough.

fettuccine

Fettuccine is one of the easiest pasta ribbons to make, besides being possibly the most popular type of egg-based pasta outside of Italy. Fettuccine are commonly found in Rome and other Central Italian areas, where they are often the pasta of choice for all sorts of sauces. This kind of pasta is very similar to Tagliatelle (page 92) but slightly wider in width. While making fettuccine, you will be able to practice all the pasta-cutting techniques explained in this chapter. You will have to make the dough quite thin, roll the sheet of pasta along its shorter edge, and slice it into ⅖-inch-wide slices using a sharp, nonserrated knife. Then you will have to delicately open up the sliced pasta and make it into a loose nest.

Once again, you don't need any special equipment to make this pasta shape—just a pasta machine or rolling pin, a knife, and your hands. Once you are confident at making fettuccine, you can easily make all sorts of pasta ribbons!

00 or all-purpose flour, for dusting

1 batch Know-by-Heart Egg Pasta Dough (page 14)

1. Dust three baking sheets with 00 or all-purpose flour.

2. Roll the dough (see page 22) and feed the prepared egg pasta sheet through the machine, adjusting the settings, until setting #7.

3. You can do this with a rolling pin, too. Make the dough as thin and uniform as possible.

4. Cut the sheet of pasta into a 6-by-10-inch-long sheet and dust it with flour. Let it rest for 5 minutes.

5. Roll the sheet of pasta along its shorter edge.

6. Using a sharp, nonserrated knife, slice it into ⅖-inch-wide slices.

7. Delicately open up the sliced pasta with your hands, dust with a little flour, and make it into a loose nest.

8. Transfer to the prepared baking sheets.

9. Repeat the above steps until you have no dough left.

making stuffed pasta

The majority of stuffed pasta is made by using egg-based pasta dough, but there are some exceptions to this rule, especially in Southern Italy. Sardinian Culurgiones (page 145) is an example—this stuffed pasta is made with durum wheat-based dough.

There are many different stuffed pasta shapes, so many that you could say each Italian city has its own characteristic shape. Bologna, for example, is famous for its Tortellini (page 140), while Bergamo is renowned for its Casoncelli (page 131), and so on. Another interesting tidbit is that while the stuffing is often interchangeable, some local shapes have a very traditional filling. Ravioli in Milan don't usually have the same filling as ravioli in Mantua, where they are known as *tortelli* and are filled with pumpkin. The reason is simple: People would make do with whatever ingredients they had available locally, and with time, these necessities were turned into traditions. Clever, right?

There are many tools available on the market to make stuffed pasta, but with those you can make only a few shapes. Learning how to make stuffed pasta from scratch will give you the flexibility to try out different recipes and shapes.

Making stuffed pasta requires you to put in practice the pasta-rolling expertise you have already acquired and to learn a few extra skills. Nothing too complicated, though, so don't worry! Let's go through all the steps together.

ROLLING

The pasta sheets to make stuffed pasta must be very thin: You want the stuffing to shine and not the pasta itself. Stuffed pasta is often folded to encase the stuffing, which means there can be two or more layers of pasta in certain parts. To make sure the pasta cooks where it's thicker, you want the pasta to be quite thin to begin with. The majority of stuffed pasta is rolled until setting #8 of the pasta machine, and it is thinner than ribbon-shaped pasta.

BE ORGANIZED
Homemade pasta dries out quite quickly. Besides making sure to keep your dough covered in plastic wrap at all times when you are not working with it, make sure to have everything you need—a knife, the stuffing, a little bowl with water—ready so you don't waste precious time after having rolled the dough.

FLOUR
When working with stuffed pasta, make sure to always dust the work surface with flour. No matter how dry your stuffing looks, it will make the dough moist, and if you forget to dust the work surface with flour, your pasta will likely stick where it shouldn't.

DRYING
Turn the stuffed pasta over a few times while drying it, or the bottom will become wet and soggy, and it may even tear.

LEFTOVER DOUGH
Gather all the leftover dough you get after cutting out the stuffed pasta shapes, make it into a ball, and roll it again to make more pasta.

STUFFING & CUTTING

Once you have rolled the dough into the required thickness, you will have to cut it into specific shapes and then fill it and seal it; or simply place your stuffing on the rolled sheet of pasta, seal it, and then cut it into your chosen shape. Make small balls with the stuffing and put them on the pasta. Make sure to leave enough space around the filling so you can close your pasta securely.

SEALING

Sealing the pasta is the most delicate part. If you don't seal it well enough, the pasta will open up when you cook it and the stuffing will come out of it, turning your masterpiece into a mess. Use some water to wet the sides of the dough to help the pasta stick better, and press well all around the stuffing with your fingers or with a fork. Make sure not to leave any air bubbles inside, or the pasta will come apart.

ravioli

Ravioli are one of the most famous kinds of stuffed pasta. You can find ravioli throughout Italy, sometimes with different names—like Mantua's tortelli. Ravioli are also one of the easiest (and quickest) stuffed pasta shapes to make, so they are perfect for beginners. All the techniques on stuffed pasta that have been covered above are used for making this pasta shape. You will have to make the dough very thin and put it on the floured work surface. You will need to take small amounts of stuffing, make them into little balls, and put them on the lower half of the sheet of pasta, leaving some space in between them. You will use your fingers to wet the sides of the dough with a little water to help the pasta stick. You will fold the other half of the sheet onto the filling, pressing well all around the stuffing to seal the pasta. After that, you will cut around the stuffing in a square shape to obtain your ravioli. Once you are satisfied with the way you make ravioli, you will find that making other stuffed pasta shapes will not feel as intimidating!

00 or all-purpose flour, for dusting

1 batch Know-by-Heart Egg Pasta Dough (page 14)

1. Dust three baking sheets with 00 or all-purpose flour.

2. Roll the dough (see page 22) and feed the prepared egg pasta sheet through the machine, adjusting the settings, until setting #8.

3. You can do this with a rolling pin, too. Make the dough as thin and uniform as possible.

4. Dust your work surface with flour and put your rolled dough on it.

continued >

FIGURE 3.7

FIGURE 3.8

FIGURE 3.9

5. Make small (hazelnut-sized) balls with the stuffing and put them on the lower half of the sheet of pasta (Figure 3.7). Make sure to leave some space in between the balls of stuffing so that you can seal the pasta well.

6. Wet the sides of the dough with a little water to help it seal.

7. Fold the other half of the sheet over the filling and press well all around (Figure 3.8). Make sure not to leave any air bubbles inside, or the pasta will open while cooking and the filling will come out.

8. Using a crinkle-edge pastry wheel or a pizza cutter, cut around the filling in a squarish shape, and remove the excess dough (Figure 3.9).

9. Transfer to the prepared baking sheets.

10. Repeat the above steps until you have no dough left.

drying pasta

Drying your freshly made pasta is not necessary. You can make it and eat it within a few minutes. However, drying becomes necessary if you want to store the pasta for later usage.

Let's go through the easy steps of the drying technique together.

DRYING

After shaping your pasta, you can leave it out to dry on your kitchen counter.

If you make short pasta, like Garganelli (page 74) or Cavatelli (page 46), you can transfer it to a pasta frame fitted with mesh (see page 9) so that the air circulates from all sides, including the bottom, and the pasta dries out uniformly. Keep your pasta spread out, rather than clumped together, so it dries faster. If using a normal tray or a baking sheet, you will have to regularly rotate the pasta so that it dries on all sides.

To dry long pasta, it is best to hang it on a pasta drying rack (see page 38). Hang the pasta immediately after unfolding it instead of making it into a loose nest. In this case, you will need to keep the strands separate so that they dry evenly.

Let the pasta dry for about 15 hours (the exact time will depend on the humidity of the air and the shape and thickness of the pasta).

AIR QUALITY

Keep the pasta in a dry but ventilated place so that it can dry without forming a superficial crust that will keep it damp on the inside.

COOKING

If you dry the pasta, you will have to cook it for a longer time to rehydrate it. Remember to always taste your pasta to make sure it's cooked through but still al dente.

NO DRYING RACK OR FRAME?
Pasta drying racks are easily available and not too expensive, but any clean rod will do. A clothes drying rack, the back of a chair, or even a hanger will work just fine.

Use a baking sheet, a tray, or a wire rack instead of a pasta frame for short pasta. Make sure to turn the pasta over if needed.

OVEN:
Pasta can also be dried more quickly by putting it on a baking sheet on the middle rack of a fan-forced oven, with the door ajar, at 100°F for about 30 minutes. However, be careful when trying this. Every oven is different and you may have to experiment with yours to find the perfect temperature.

FRAGILE!
Be gentle with the pasta once it has dried, because it will be brittle and could break.

STORING

If dried correctly, homemade pasta can be stored in paper bags in your pantry for up to one month.

If you'd like to freeze the pasta, be sure to dry it completely before placing it in freezer-safe, resealable plastic bags. If it remains moist, it may get moldy. Pasta will keep in the freezer for up to two months.

Fresh pasta can be stored, after drying for about 30 minutes, in plastic bags in the refrigerator for up to 12 hours.

All pasta can be dried, but not all of it can be stored for a long time. Stuffed pasta should be consumed within a day, unless frozen.

how to dry fettuccine

Follow these simple steps to apply and practice all the techniques you have learned about drying pasta. Remember that you can do the same thing with other kinds of pasta, such as short and/or hand-shaped pasta. For these types, use a pasta frame instead of a drying rack.

1 batch Fettuccine (page 90)

1. As soon as you cut your fettuccine, hang the ribbons on a pasta drying rack to dry.

2. Keep the pasta strands separate and with space between them, so that they dry evenly.

3. Let the pasta dry for about 15 hours, or until completely dry. Keep the pasta in a dry, aerated place.

4. Carefully remove the dried fettuccine from the rack and transfer them to paper bags or freezer-safe, resealable plastic bags.

5. Store for up to one month in your pantry or two months in the freezer.

cooking pasta

Now that you know how to make your pasta, let's learn how to cook it in the correct way. You wouldn't want to overcook it and ruin all your hard work, would you?

COOKING

To cook pasta correctly, you need a large pot of water—about 5 quarts. Bring the water to a boil and add 1½ tablespoons of sea salt. When the water is boiling, add the pasta and stir. Cook, stirring occasionally with a wooden spoon to stop the pasta from sticking to the bottom of the pot. There is no need to add oil to the water, as this would stop the sauce from clinging to the cooked pasta.

Always cook your pasta al dente. There is nothing worse than overcooked pasta, since it becomes slippery and begins to break. Use the cooking times listed in this book as a reference only. The times have been given for freshly made pasta. If you let your pasta dry (see page 37), it will take longer to cook. The exact cooking time will also vary slightly depending on the thickness of the pasta.

TASTING

The only infallible way to cook the perfect pasta is to taste it before draining it: Remove a piece of pasta from the pot and take a bite. It should be cooked but still slightly firm in the center: *Perfetto!*

DRAINING

Depending on the pasta, you will need to drain it by using either a colander or a slotted spoon. Gnocchi and stuffed pastas, which are more delicate, are best drained with a slotted spoon. You will find this information listed with each recipe.

MIXING WITH THE SAUCE

Depending on the sauce you choose, you can either sauté the pasta in the pot with the sauce for a minute or two, or put the pasta in a large serving bowl and toss it with the sauce. Sauces made from raw ingredients, like pesto, are best mixed with the pasta in a serving bowl to prevent them from cooking and turning black. You will find this information along with each recipe, when required.

what's next?

Now that you are armed with your easy pasta dough recipes and have experimented with some (or all) of the tutorials in this chapter, you are more than ready to work your way through the pasta recipes in Part 2. You will be able to try making various hand-shaped pasta, pasta ribbons, stuffed pasta, gnocchi, and gnudi. Unsure of what sauce to serve them with? Fear not, as I've got you covered! You will find recipes for delightful sauces to serve with your handmade pasta, including tips and serving suggestions. So, are you ready? Let's start cooking!

the recipes

N ow it's finally time to put all you have learned so far to the test. Isn't it exciting? In this part of the book you will find recipes for how to make hand-shaped pasta, ribbon pasta, stuffed pasta—stuffing included—gnocchi, and gnudi. You will be gradually introduced to more complex shapes and tutorials, since the recipes have been organized from easier to more challenging within each chapter to keep building on your skills.

The last chapter is all about sauces, which, far from being a trivial subject, is essential to the art of good pasta making. You can make the best-looking pappardelle, but if you pair it with the wrong sauce, your dish will not fare well. Besides sharing the recipes for authentic and scrumptious Italian pasta sauces, I will give you pairing tips and serving suggestions that will have your family and friends craving more.

chapter 4

HAND-SHAPED PASTA

THE ART OF HAND-SHAPING PASTA is an ancient one, and it still lives on in many Italian households, especially in the South of the country. When visiting small towns and villages, it is common to find old ladies kneading and transforming pasta dough into beautifully crafted pasta at a speed that can hardly be believed. It takes time and lots of practice to get as good as that, but we can take our time and enjoy the learning experience.

In this chapter, you will find recipes and tutorials on how to make some of the most popular types of hand-shaped pasta. We will start from relatively easy shapes, like Cavatelli (page 46), Cavatellini (page 48), and Cicatelli (page 50). As you get more confident with your shaping skills, we will progressively move on to more complicated shapes, like Fusilli Avelli-nesi (page 68), Orecchiette (page 72), and Garganelli (page 74). Even though you will be required to use a few tools, like a knitting needle and a gnocchi board, the majority of the work will be done using your hands.

<< LEFT: ORECCHIETTE (PAGE 72) WITH KALE, GORGONZOLA, AND GREEN PESTO (PAGE 210)

cavatelli

 Cavatelli are short, narrow pasta shells with crinkled edges that curve inward a bit. This type of pasta is usually made in the Southern Italian regions of Campania, Molise, Apulia, and Basilicata. The name comes from the Italian word *cavo*, which means "hollow," and the pasta is thus called because of its hollow shape. This is a very simple pasta shape that requires no special equipment. **SERVES 4**

PREP TIME: 1 HOUR AND 15 MINUTES | **COOK TIME:** 6 TO 8 MINUTES

EQUIPMENT

Knife, nonserrated

3 (10-by-15-inch) baking sheets

Large pot, to cook the pasta

Wooden spoon, to stir the pasta

Colander, to drain the pasta

INGREDIENTS

Durum wheat flour, for dusting

1 batch Know-by-Heart Durum Wheat Pasta Dough (page 16)

Sea salt, for cooking the pasta

TO MAKE THE PASTA

1. Dust the baking sheets with durum wheat flour.

2. Break the dough into several 3-inch balls and roll them into ⅔-inch-thick ropes using your fingertips.

3. Cut these ropes into 1-inch-long pieces.

4. Put your index and middle fingers together and press them down on each piece of dough, rolling it toward you with a quick movement.

5. Put the shaped pasta on the prepared baking sheets.

6. Repeat the above steps until you have no dough left.

Cavatelli are traditionally served with Mussel and Bean Sauce (page 202), Spicy Pork Ragù (page 212), Crudaiola Sauce (page 176), Sun-dried Tomato Sauce (page 181), or Arugula and Tomato Sauce (page 196). All these sauces are commonly made in Campania, Molise, Apulia, and Basilicata, just like cavatelli.

TO COOK THE PASTA

1. Set a large pot of salted water on the stove to boil (see page 40). Cook the pasta in the boiling water for 6 to 8 minutes, or until al dente. To test this, remove a piece of pasta from the pot and take a bite. It should be cooked but still slightly firm in the center.

2. When the pasta is ready, drain it through a colander and shake out the excess water.

3. Serve immediately with the sauce of your choice.

TIP: Make sure your cavatelli are cooked by tasting them before draining. The exact time will depend on the pressure you apply to the dough when shaping them: The more pressure applied, the thinner your cavatelli will be and the less time they will need to cook.

cavatellini

 Cavatellini are small cavatelli made using only the index finger. Unlike cavatelli, which are typically served with thick or dry sauces, cavatellini are usually served in soups often made with chickpeas, beans, and lentils. They are a specialty from the Southern region of Apulia. **SERVES 4**

PREP TIME: 1 HOUR AND 15 MINUTES | **COOK TIME:** 6 TO 8 MINUTES

EQUIPMENT

Knife, nonserrated

3 (10-by-15-inch) baking sheets

Large pot, to cook the pasta

Wooden spoon, to stir the pasta

Colander, to drain the pasta

INGREDIENTS

Durum wheat flour, for dusting

1 batch Know-by-Heart Durum Wheat Pasta Dough (page 16)

Sea salt, for cooking the pasta

TO MAKE THE PASTA

1. Dust the baking sheets with durum wheat flour.

2. Break the dough into about 3-inch balls and roll them into ⅔-inch-thick ropes using your fingertips.

3. Cut these ropes into ½-inch-long pieces.

4. Press your index finger down on each piece of dough, rolling it toward you with a quick movement.

5. Put the shaped pasta on the prepared baking sheets.

6. Repeat the above steps until you have no dough left.

Cavatellini are usually served with soups, such as Chickpea Soup (page 204), but can also be eaten with a simple Tomato and Basil Sauce (page 182).

TO COOK THE PASTA

1. Set a large pot of salted water on the stove to boil (see page 40). Cook the pasta in the boiling water for 6 to 8 minutes, or until al dente. To test this, remove a piece of pasta from the pot and take a bite. It should be cooked but still slightly firm in the center.

2. When the pasta is ready, drain it through a colander and shake out the excess water.

3. Serve immediately with the sauce of your choice.

TIP: When making cavatellini with soups, I suggest you cook them in the soup itself. This will enhance the final flavor, and the starch released by the pasta will thicken the soup. Make sure the soup has enough liquid to cook the pasta without becoming dry.

cicatelli

Cicatelli are longer cavatelli and are made using three fingers instead of two. They are a specialty from the Southern region of Apulia. They can be served with fish, meat, and vegetarian sauces, and they are probably the most versatile hand-shaped pasta of all. I personally prefer them with strongly flavored or spicy sauces, but the choice is yours. SERVES 4

PREP TIME: 1 HOUR AND 15 MINUTES | **COOK TIME:** 6 TO 8 MINUTES

EQUIPMENT

Knife, nonserrated

3 (10-by-15-inch) baking sheets

Large pot, to cook the pasta

Wooden spoon, to stir the pasta

Colander, to drain the pasta

INGREDIENTS

Durum wheat flour, for dusting

1 batch Know-by-Heart Durum Wheat Pasta Dough (page 16)

Sea salt, for cooking the pasta

TO MAKE THE PASTA

1. Dust the baking sheets with durum wheat flour.

2. Break the dough into 2-inch balls and roll them into ½-inch-thick ropes using your fingertips.

3. Cut these ropes into 1½-inch-long pieces.

4. Put your index, middle, and ring fingers together and press them down on each piece of dough, rolling it toward you with a quick movement.

5. Put the shaped pasta on the prepared baking sheets.

6. Repeat the above steps until you have no dough left.

Cicatelli can be served with Prawn and Zucchini Sauce (page 187), Arugula and Tomato Sauce (page 196), Crudaiola Sauce (page 176), or Arrabbiata Sauce (page 195).

TO COOK THE PASTA

1. Set a large pot of salted water on the stove to boil (see page 40). Cook the pasta in the boiling water for 6 to 8 minutes, or until al dente. To test this, remove a piece of pasta from the pot and take a bite. It should be cooked but still slightly firm in the center.

2. When the pasta is ready, drain it through a colander and shake out the excess water.

3. Serve immediately with the sauce of your choice.

TIP: When making cicatelli, lightly dust your fingers with durum wheat flour so that the dough does not stick to your hand. Do not dust the ropes of dough with flour, or they will slip and you will not be able to shape them.

farfalle

Farfalle—known in English as "bow ties"—are a traditional pasta shape from the North of Italy. The word *farfalle* means "butterflies" in Italian, and this pasta is usually a favorite among kids. Homemade farfalle are usually made with egg pasta dough. You can also make them smaller by cutting smaller squares of dough and then serve them in your favorite soups. **SERVES 4**

PREP TIME: 45 MINUTES | **COOK TIME:** 2 MINUTES

EQUIPMENT

Pasta machine or rolling pin

Crinkle-edge pastry wheel

3 (10-by-15-inch) baking sheets

Large pot, to cook the pasta

Wooden spoon, to stir the pasta

Colander, to drain the pasta

INGREDIENTS

00 or all-purpose flour, for dusting

1 batch Know-by-Heart Egg Pasta Dough (page 14), rolled

Sea salt, for cooking the pasta

TO MAKE THE PASTA

1. Dust the baking sheets with 00 or all-purpose flour.

2. Roll the dough (see page 22) and feed the prepared egg pasta sheet through a pasta machine, adjusting the settings, until setting #7. If the sheet of pasta gets too long, you can cut it in half with a knife.

3. You can do this with a rolling pin, too. Make the dough as thin and uniform as possible.

4. Using the crinkle-edge pastry wheel, cut the pasta sheets into 2½-inch squares.

5. To make bow ties, simply pinch each square in the middle with your thumb and index finger.

6. Transfer to the prepared baking sheets.

7. Repeat the above steps with the remaining dough.

Farfalle can be served with Cream Sauce with Salmon (page 191), Arugula and Tomato Sauce (page 196), Sun-dried Tomato Sauce (page 181), or Cream Sauce with Ham and Peas (page 193).

TO COOK THE PASTA

1. Set a large pot of salted water on the stove to boil (see page 40). Cook the pasta for about 2 minutes, or until al dente. To test this, remove a piece of pasta from the pot and take a bite. It should be cooked but still slightly firm in the center.

2. When the pasta is ready, drain it through a colander and shake out the excess water.

3. Serve immediately with the sauce of your choice.

TIP: If you prefer, you can also make straight-edged farfalle. Simply use a knife or a pizza cutter to cut out the pasta squares before pinching them in the middle.

pici

Pici are thick, hand-rolled pasta strands, similar to chunky spaghetti. This type of pasta originates in the province of Siena, in Tuscany. I remember eating it with a wild boar sauce a few years ago when I visited the area, and it was love at first bite. It is a very rustic and hearty kind of pasta, so it goes very well with meat-based sauces or sauces with a strong flavor. **SERVES 4**

PREP TIME: 1 HOUR AND 15 MINUTES | **COOK TIME:** 8 TO 10 MINUTES

EQUIPMENT

Rolling pin

Pizza cutter

3 (10-by-15-inch) baking sheets

Large pot, to cook the pasta

Wooden spoon, to stir the pasta

Colander, to drain the pasta

INGREDIENTS

Durum wheat flour, for dusting

1 batch Know-by-Heart Durum Wheat Pasta Dough (page 16)

Sea salt, for cooking the pasta

TO MAKE THE PASTA

1. Dust the baking sheets with durum wheat flour.

2. Using a rolling pin, roll the dough into a ⅓-inch-thick rectangular sheet.

3. With a pizza cutter, cut out ⅓-inch-wide strips.

4. Roll these strips into ⅕- to ⅖-inch-thick ropes using your fingertips, making them as uniform as possible.

5. Cut these ropes into long pieces, up to 11 inches long.

6. Coat the pici well with durum wheat flour, so they do not stick.

7. Put the shaped pasta on the prepared baking sheets.

8. Repeat the above steps until you have no dough left.

serving suggestion

Pici are traditionally served with Aglione Sauce (page 194), as both the pasta shape and the sauce come from Tuscany. However, they also go very well with Bucaiola Sauce (page 178), Arrabbiata Sauce (page 195), or Ragù alla Bolognese (page 216).

TO COOK THE PASTA

1. Set a large pot of salted water on the stove to boil (see page 40). Cook the pasta for about 8 to 10 minutes, or until al dente. To test this, remove a piece of pasta from the pot and take a bite. It should be cooked but still slightly firm in the center.

2. When the pasta is ready, drain it through a colander and shake out the excess water.

3. Serve immediately with the sauce of your choice.

TIP: You can also make pici with all-purpose flour instead of durum wheat flour. Keep the water-to-flour ratio the same as in the durum wheat dough recipe. Using all-purpose flour will make it easier to roll pici thin. Knead the dough very well to make it more elastic. Taste the pasta before draining, as the cooking time may be different.

malloreddus

Malloreddus come from the beautiful Italian island of Sardinia. The word *malloreddu* means "baby calf" in Campidanese, one of the local Sardinian languages. I know it seems like a strange name for a shape of pasta, but among the locals, calves have always been seen as a sign of abundance, especially if well fed, and the shape of this pasta is rounded, just like a fatted calf. Malloreddus are also known as *gnocchetti Sardi*—little Sardinian gnocchi—as they are shaped like gnocchi, the only difference being the dough. SERVES 4

PREP TIME: 1 HOUR AND 15 MINUTES | **COOK TIME:** 6 TO 8 MINUTES

EQUIPMENT

Wooden gnocchi board or fork

Knife, nonserrated

3 (10-by-15-inch) baking sheets

Large pot, to cook the pasta

Wooden spoon, to stir the pasta

Colander, to drain the pasta

INGREDIENTS

Durum wheat flour, for dusting

1 batch Know-by-Heart Durum Wheat Pasta Dough (page 16)

Sea salt, for cooking the pasta

TO MAKE THE PASTA

1. Dust the baking sheets with durum wheat flour.

2. Break the dough into about 3-inch balls and roll them into ⅖-inch-thick ropes using your fingertips.

3. Cut these ropes into 1-inch-long pieces.

4. Shape them like gnocchi by rolling them on the tines of a fork (or on a gnocchi board) while pressing down with your thumb.

5. Put the shaped pasta on the prepared baking sheets.

6. Repeat the above steps until you have no dough left.

Malloreddus can be served with meat or vegetable sauces. Traditionally they are served with Sausage Sauce (page 214), a recipe that uses local ingredients, but I also like them with Spicy Pork Ragù (page 212).

TO COOK THE PASTA

1. Set a large pot of salted water on the stove to boil (see page 40). Cook the pasta in the boiling water for 6 to 8 minutes, or until al dente. To test this, remove a piece of pasta from the pot and take a bite. It should be cooked but still slightly firm in the center.

2. When the pasta is ready, drain it through a colander and shake out the excess water.

3. Serve immediately with the sauce of your choice.

TIP: You can add a pinch of saffron powder to the durum wheat dough when making malloreddus. Just dissolve the saffron in the water you use for kneading the dough for a vibrantly yellow color. This is how malloreddus were originally made, and it also adds a subtle flavor. Don't overdo it, though. Only a pinch is needed! Another option is to add the saffron and 1 garlic clove to Sausage Sauce (page 214).

cozzette

 Cozzette are durum wheat pasta shapes traditionally made in the Southern Italian region of Apulia. Their Italian name means "little mussels", as their shape is similar to the small mussels that abound in the area. This pasta is really easy to make, and it goes especially well with fish-based sauces. **SERVES 4**

PREP TIME: 1 HOUR AND 15 MINUTES | **COOK TIME:** 5 MINUTES

EQUIPMENT

Big wooden board or big wooden cutting board

Table knife, round edged

3 (10-by-15-inch) baking sheets

Large pot, to cook the pasta

Wooden spoon, to stir the pasta

Colander, to drain the pasta

INGREDIENTS

Durum wheat flour, for dusting

1 batch Know-by-Heart Durum Wheat Pasta Dough (page 16)

Sea salt, for cooking the pasta

TO MAKE THE PASTA

1. Dust the baking sheets with durum wheat flour.

2. Work on a wooden surface to give cozzette their traditional "wrinkled" texture.

3. Break the dough into about 3-inch balls and roll them into ⅖-inch-thick ropes using your fingertips.

4. Cut these ropes into ¾-inch-long pieces.

5. Holding a table knife at a 45-degree angle to the work surface, press and roll the dough toward you. Now you have shaped your "mussel."

6. Put the shaped pasta on the prepared baking sheets.

7. Repeat the above steps until you have no dough left.

Cozzette are traditionally served with Prawn and Zucchini Sauce (page 187) or Mussel and Bean Sauce (page 202), as seafood is very easily found in the area where cozzette come from. However, a simple Tomato and Basil Sauce (page 182) works well, too.

TO COOK THE PASTA

1. Set a large pot of salted water on the stove to boil (see page 40). Cook the pasta for about 5 minutes, or until al dente. To test this, remove a piece of pasta from the pot and take a bite. It should be cooked but still slightly firm in the center.

2. When the pasta is ready, drain it through a colander and shake out the excess water.

3. Serve immediately with the sauce of your choice.

TIP: To make cozzette, make sure to use a knife with a rounded edge, so that when you use it to press and roll the dough, the pasta will not tear and your shapes will come out perfect.

strascinati

Strascinati (or *strascinate*) are traditionally made in the Southern regions of Italy, especially Apulia and Basilicata. Their name means "pulled," because you need to pull the dough to give them their characteristic shape. They are similar to orecchiette but are bigger and flatter; this is because unlike orecchiette, they are not flipped inside out after being pulled with the knife. SERVES 4

PREP TIME: 1 HOUR AND 15 MINUTES | **COOK TIME:** 5 MINUTES

EQUIPMENT

Big wooden board or big wooden cutting board

Knife, nonserrated

Metal cake spatula

3 (10-by-15-inch) baking sheets

Large pot, to cook the pasta

Wooden spoon, to stir the pasta

Colander, to drain the pasta

INGREDIENTS

Durum wheat flour, for dusting

1 batch Know-by-Heart Durum Wheat Pasta Dough (page 16)

Sea salt, for cooking the pasta

TO MAKE THE PASTA

1. Dust the baking sheets with durum wheat flour.

2. Work on a wooden surface to give strascinati their traditional "wrinkled" texture.

3. Break the dough into about 3-inch balls and roll them into ⅔-inch-thick ropes using your fingertips.

4. Cut these ropes into 1-inch-long pieces.

5. Holding a metal cake spatula at a 45-degree angle to the work surface, press and roll the dough toward you, while holding the top part of the pasta with the other hand, so the strascinato does not curl.

6. Put the shaped pasta on the prepared baking sheets.

7. Repeat the above steps until you have no dough left.

Strascinati are usually served with Broccoli Rabe Sauce (page 199), Arugula and Tomato Sauce (page 196), Crudaiola Sauce (page 176), Kale, Gorgonzola, and Green Pesto (page 210), or a simple Tomato and Basil Sauce (page 182).

TO COOK THE PASTA

1. Set a large pot of salted water on the stove to boil (see page 40). Cook the pasta for about 5 minutes, or until al dente. To test this, remove a piece of pasta from the pot and take a bite. It should be cooked but still slightly firm in the center.

2. When the pasta is ready, drain it through a colander and shake out the excess water.

3. Serve immediately with the sauce of your choice.

TIP: Strascinati are traditionally made using a specific tool called a *rasula*. This tool looks like a small metal dough scraper with a long handle. If you do not have one, you can use a metal cake spatula.

trofie

Trofie are a shape of short pasta typical of Liguria, in Northern Italy. This pasta is very easy to make, as it requires only the palm of your hand and two basic moves to shape it. It is so easy to make that my kids usually help me out! It has always been my absolute favorite pasta to make and eat. **SERVES 4**

PREP TIME: 1 HOUR AND 15 MINUTES | **COOK TIME:** 5 MINUTES

EQUIPMENT

3 (10-by-15-inch) baking sheets

Large pot, to cook the pasta

Wooden spoon, to stir the pasta

Colander, to drain the pasta

INGREDIENTS

Durum wheat flour, for dusting

1 batch Know-by-Heart Durum Wheat Pasta Dough (page 16)

Sea salt, for cooking the pasta

TO MAKE THE PASTA

1. Dust the baking sheets with durum wheat flour.

2. Take small balls of dough (about ⅔ inch) and roll them using your palm into small ropes about 1½ inches long. Make sure the ends of the ropes are thinner than the middle part.

3. Put the side of your hand perpendicular to the left end of the rope of pasta and pull it toward you while applying a light pressure. This motion will twirl the pasta, giving it its characteristic shape.

4. Put the shaped pasta on the prepared baking sheets.

5. Repeat the above steps until you have no dough left.

Trofie are traditionally served with Pesto alla Genovese (page 183) or Walnut Sauce (page 179), both of which are from the region of Liguria.

TO COOK THE PASTA

1. Set a large pot of salted water on the stove to boil (see page 40). Cook the pasta for about 5 minutes, or until al dente. To test this, remove a piece of pasta from the pot and take a bite. It should be cooked but still slightly firm in the center.

2. When the pasta is ready, drain it through a colander and shake out the excess water.

3. Serve immediately with the sauce of your choice.

TIP: When making trofie, do not dust your work surface with flour or your trofie will slip and will not twirl properly. If required, you can also dampen your hands slightly to make them less slippery.

strozzapreti

Strozzapreti are a traditional hand-rolled pasta shape from the Romagna area of Emilia-Romagna. The name translates to "priest chokers," and there are many legends about why this pasta has such a peculiar name. A possible explanation could be the fact that this pasta was made by local women as partial payment to the priests for land rents (in Romagna, the Catholic Church used to have extensive land properties rented to farmers). This would make the farmers so angry that they wished the priests could choke while eating the pasta. The name surely reflects the diffuse anticlericalism of the people of Romagna. However, fear not, as nobody really chokes when eating strozzapreti. It is in fact a delicious shape of pasta that goes really well with all kinds of sauces! **SERVES 4**

PREP TIME: 1 HOUR AND 15 MINUTES | **COOK TIME:** 2 MINUTES

EQUIPMENT

Rolling pin

3 (10-by-15-inch) baking sheets

Knife, nonserrated, or pizza cutter

Large pot, to cook the pasta

Wooden spoon, to stir the pasta

Colander, to drain the pasta

INGREDIENTS

Durum wheat flour, for dusting

1 batch Know-by-Heart Durum Wheat Pasta Dough (page 16)

Sea salt, for cooking the pasta

TO MAKE THE PASTA

1. Dust the baking sheets with durum wheat flour.

2. Using a rolling pin, roll the dough into a 1/10-inch-thick rectangular sheet.

3. With a knife or pizza cutter, cut out 3/4-inch-wide strips.

4. Take one strip and put the top of it between your hands. Roll the pasta between your palms to twirl it.

5. Pinch and break it into 3½-inch-long pieces.

6. Put the shaped pasta on the prepared baking sheets.

7. Repeat the above steps until you have no dough left.

serving suggestion

Strozzapreti are traditionally served with seafood sauces, like Prawn and Zucchini Sauce (page 187), as seafood is a staple in Romagna, but they also go very well with Arrabbiata Sauce (page 195) or Ragù alla Bolognese (page 216).

TO COOK THE PASTA

1. Set a large pot of salted water on the stove to boil (see page 40). Cook the pasta in the boiling water for about 2 minutes, or until al dente. To test this, remove a piece of pasta from the pot and take a bite. It should be cooked but still slightly firm in the center.

2. When the pasta is ready, drain it through a colander and shake out the excess water.

3. Serve immediately with the sauce of your choice.

TIP: There is no need to be very precise when making strozzapreti. It is a very rustic kind of pasta. The only thing to watch out for is the thickness. Try and roll all the dough uniformly, so all the pasta will have the same cooking time.

maccheroni col ferretto

Maccheroni col Ferretto are traditional durum wheat–based pasta that can be found throughout Southern Italy. They are made by rolling pieces of dough around a special metal skewer called a *ferretto*. If you do not have a ferretto, you can use a knitting needle instead. The resulting shape is a hollow and straight cylinder that goes very well with spicy and tomato-based sauces. **SERVES 4**

PREP TIME: 1 HOUR AND 15 MINUTES | **COOK TIME:** 5 MINUTES

EQUIPMENT

Knitting needle, size 0 or 1

Knife, nonserrated

3 (10-by-15-inch) baking sheets

Large pot, to cook the pasta

Wooden spoon, to stir the pasta

Colander, to drain the pasta

INGREDIENTS

Durum wheat flour, for dusting

1 batch Know-by-Heart Durum Wheat Pasta Dough (page 16)

Sea salt, for cooking the pasta

TO MAKE THE PASTA

1. Dust the baking sheets with durum wheat flour.

2. Break the dough into about 2-inch balls and roll them into ⅓-inch-thick ropes using your fingertips.

3. Cut these ropes into 1¼-inch-long pieces.

4. Lay one of the cut ropes on the work surface and place the knitting needle horizontally on the top. Press down on the knitting needle slightly with the palm of your hand, so that it sticks to the dough.

5. Roll the knitting needle over the rope so that the rope rolls up around it.

Maccheroni col Ferretto are usually served with Spicy Pork Ragù (page 212), Arrabbiata Sauce (page 195), or a simple Tomato and Basil Sauce (page 182), all tomato-based sauces that go really well with such a rustic pasta shape.

6. Gently roll it back and forth with your hand to make the pasta longer and thinner.

7. Carefully, slide the pasta off of the knitting needle with your hand, while preserving the shape.

8. Put the shaped pasta on the prepared baking sheets.

9. Repeat the above steps until you have no dough left.

TO COOK THE PASTA

1. Set a large pot of salted water on the stove to boil (see page 40). Cook the pasta for about 5 minutes, or until al dente. To test this, remove a piece of pasta from the pot and take a bite. It should be cooked but still slightly firm in the center.

2. When the pasta is ready, drain it through a colander and shake out the excess water.

3. Serve immediately with the sauce of your choice.

TIP: When shaping maccheroni col ferretto, make sure that the knitting needle is parallel to the piece of dough. This will ensure that the pasta gets the hollow but straight shape it is so famous for.

fusilli avellinesi

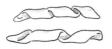 Fusilli Avellinesi are a traditional corkscrew-shaped pasta from the town of Avellino, in the Campania region. Like Busiati (page 70), it is made using a knitting needle, but fusilli are usually shorter. The term *fusillo* comes from the word *fuso*, which means "spindle," as the technique used to shape the pasta around the knitting needle is similar to the one used to spin yarn using a spindle. **SERVES 4**

PREP TIME: 1 HOUR AND 15 MINUTES | **COOK TIME:** 6 TO 8 MINUTES

EQUIPMENT

Knitting needle, size 0 or 1

Knife, nonserrated

3 (10-by-15-inch) baking sheets

Large pot, to cook the pasta

Wooden spoon, to stir the pasta

Colander, to drain the pasta

INGREDIENTS

Durum wheat flour, for dusting

1 batch Know-by-Heart Durum Wheat Pasta Dough (page 16)

Sea salt, for cooking the pasta

TO MAKE THE PASTA

1. Dust the baking sheets with durum wheat flour.

2. Break the dough into about 2-inch balls and roll them into ½-inch-thick ropes using your fingertips.

3. Cut these ropes into 2-inch-long pieces.

4. Keep the cut ropes horizontal and place the middle part of the knitting needle at a 45-degree angle on the right end of the piece of dough. Press the knitting needle slightly with the palm of your hand, so that it sticks to the dough.

5. Roll the knitting needle away from you at an angle with your hands, until the dough gets fully wrapped around the needle.

6. Gently roll it back and forth with your hand to make the pasta longer and thinner.

Fusilli Avellinesi are usually served with Spicy Pork Ragù (page 212) but can also be served with Pumpkin and Sausage Sauce (page 208), or a simple Tomato and Basil Sauce (page 182).

7. Carefully slide the pasta off of the knitting needle with your hand, while preserving the shape.

8. Put the shaped pasta on the prepared baking sheets.

9. Repeat the above steps until you have no dough left.

TO COOK THE PASTA

1. Set a large pot of salted water on the stove to boil (see page 40). Cook the pasta in the boiling water for 6 to 8 minutes, or until al dente. To test this, remove a piece of pasta from the pot and take a bite. It should be cooked, but still slightly firm in the center.

2. When the pasta is ready, drain it through a colander and shake out the excess water.

3. Serve immediately with the sauce of your choice.

TIP: Regulate the pressure of your hand when rolling your fusilli around the knitting needle to make them all of the same thickness. This will ensure that they cook uniformly and all at the same time.

busiati

Busiati (also known as *busiate*) are a traditional hand-shaped pasta from the Sicilian town of Trapani. Like other shapes commonly found in Southern Italy, such as Fusilli Avellinisi (page 68), this one is made using a knitting needle. Busiati are usually longer than fusilli. I learned how to make busiati in the Sicilian town of San Vito Lo Capo, where a local old lady taught me the art of rolling busiati by hand. The name of this pasta comes from the word *buso*, which is the name of a wooden stick from a plant that grows in abundance locally. The buso is what was traditionally used to shape busiati instead of the knitting needle. SERVES 4

PREP TIME: 1 HOUR AND 15 MINUTES | **COOK TIME:** 6 TO 8 MINUTES

EQUIPMENT

Knitting needle, size 0 or 1

Knife, nonserrated

3 (10-by-15-inch) baking sheets

Large pot, to cook the pasta

Wooden spoon, to stir the pasta

Colander, to drain the pasta

INGREDIENTS

Durum wheat flour, for dusting

1 batch Know-by-Heart Durum Wheat Pasta Dough (page 16)

Sea salt, for cooking the pasta

TO MAKE THE PASTA

1. Dust the baking sheets with durum wheat flour.

2. Break the dough into about 2-inch balls and roll them into ½-inch-thick ropes using your fingertips.

3. Cut these ropes into 5-inch-long pieces.

4. Keep the cut ropes horizontal and place the middle part of the knitting needle at a 45-degree angle on the right end of the piece of dough (Figure 4.1). Press the knitting needle slightly with the palm of your hand, so that it sticks to the dough.

5. Roll the knitting needle away from you at an angle with your hands, until the dough gets fully wrapped around the needle.

6. Gently roll it back and forth with your hand to make the pasta longer and thinner.

Busiati are traditionally served with Pesto alla Trapanese (page 185) or with a simple Tomato and Basil Sauce (page 182). Both sauces are a staple in the area of Trapani, where busiati were created. Treat your taste buds to a complete Sicilian experience by serving busiati with slices of fried eggplant and grated Pecorino Romano on the top.

FIGURE 4.1

7. Carefully slide the pasta off of the knitting needle with your hand, while preserving the shape.

8. Put the shaped pasta on the prepared baking sheets.

9. Repeat the above steps until you have no dough left.

TO COOK THE PASTA

1. Set a large pot of salted water on the stove to boil (see page 40). Cook the pasta in the boiling water for 6 to 8 minutes, or until al dente. To test this, remove a piece of pasta from the pot and take a bite. It should be cooked but still slightly firm in the center.

2. When the pasta is ready, drain it through a colander and shake out the excess water.

3. Serve immediately with the sauce of your choice.

TIP: When shaping busiati, make sure to lightly dust the ropes of dough with durum wheat flour before rolling them. If the dough sticks to the knitting needle, you will not be able to slide out the busiato without ruining its shape.

orecchiette

Orecchiette are a pasta shape traditionally made in the Southern Italian regions of Apulia and Basilicata. The term *orecchiette* literally means "little ears"—their shape is similar to the ears of a baby. Making orecchiette is easier than it seems, and you do not require any special equipment: All you need is a wooden surface, a knife, and a little bit of practice! SERVES 4

PREP TIME: 1 HOUR AND 15 MINUTES | **COOK TIME:** 5 MINUTES

EQUIPMENT

Big wooden board or big wooden cutting board

Table knife, round edged

3 (10-by-15-inch) baking sheets

Large pot, to cook the pasta

Wooden spoon, to stir the pasta

Colander, to drain the pasta

INGREDIENTS

Durum wheat flour, for dusting

1 batch Know-by-Heart Durum Wheat Pasta Dough (page 16)

Sea salt, for cooking the pasta

TO MAKE THE PASTA

1. Dust the baking sheets with durum wheat flour.

2. Work on a wooden surface to give orecchiette their traditional "wrinkled" texture.

3. Break the dough into about 3-inch balls and roll them into ⅔-inch-thick ropes using your fingertips.

4. Cut these ropes into ¾-inch-long pieces.

5. Holding a table knife at a 45-degree angle to the work surface, press and roll the dough toward you (Figure 4.2).

serving suggestion

Orecchiette are traditionally served with Broccoli Rabe Sauce (page 199), Spicy Pork Ragù (page 212), Crudaiola Sauce (page 176), Sun-dried Tomato Sauce (page 181), or Arugula and Tomato Sauce (page 196). All these sauces are very common in Apulia and Basilicata, where orecchiette were born. However, I particularly like them with Kale, Gorgonzola, and Green Pesto (page 210).

FIGURE 4.2

FIGURE 4.3

FIGURE 4.4

FIGURE 4.5

6. Unfurl each piece of dough over your thumb in the opposite direction to form a concave shape (Figures 4.3 to 4.5). Now you have shaped your orecchietta.

7. Put the shaped pasta on the prepared baking sheets.

8. Repeat the above steps until you have no dough left.

TO COOK THE PASTA

1. Set a large pot of salted water on the stove to boil (see page 40). Cook the pasta for about 5 minutes, or until al dente. To test this, remove a piece of pasta from the pot and take a bite. It should be cooked but still slightly firm in the center.

2. When the pasta is ready, drain it through a colander and shake out the excess water.

3. Serve immediately with the sauce of your choice.

TIP: When serving orecchiette with Broccoli Rabe Sauce (page 199), reserve the water in which you have boiled the broccoli rabe and use it to cook the orecchiette. Doing this will enhance the flavor of the final dish.

garganelli

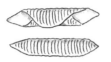 Garganelli are a traditional egg pasta shape from the Emilia-Romagna region. They are formed by rolling flat, square pieces of dough into a tubular shape. Garganelli look similar to penne, but they have an extra flap where one corner of the pasta square adheres to the other corner. Garganelli are usually made with a specific garganelli board and a mini rolling pin, but you can make them just as well using a gnocchi board or, if you don't care for the ridged surface, even without one. **SERVES 4**

PREP TIME: 1 HOUR | **COOK TIME:** 2 MINUTES

EQUIPMENT

Pasta machine or rolling pin

Knife, nonserrated

3 (10-by-15-inch) baking sheets

Gnocchi board (optional)

Large pot, to cook the pasta

Wooden spoon, to stir the pasta

Colander, to drain the pasta

INGREDIENTS

00 or all-purpose flour, for dusting

1 batch Know-by-Heart Egg Pasta Dough (page 14), rolled

Sea salt, for cooking the pasta

TO MAKE THE PASTA

1. Dust the baking sheets with 00 or all-purpose flour.

2. Roll the dough (see page 22) and feed the prepared egg pasta sheet through the machine, adjusting the settings, until setting #7. If the sheet of pasta gets too long, you can cut it in half with a knife.

3. You can do this with a rolling pin too. Make the dough as thin and uniform as possible.

4. Using a sharp knife, cut the pasta sheets into 2-inch squares.

Garganelli can be served with Cream Sauce with Salmon (page 191), Artichoke Sauce (page 197), Pumpkin and Sausage Sauce (page 208), Sun-dried Tomato Sauce (page 181), or Cream Sauce with Ham and Peas (page 193).

5. Roll the round handle of a wooden spoon from one corner to the other to make a penne-like shape. Without removing it from the wooden spoon, put the penne-like shape on a gnocchi board and roll it on the board to seal and give the pasta its characteristic ridges. If you don't have a gnocchi board, you can skip this step and simply roll the pasta on your work surface.

6. Carefully slide the garganello off the wooden spoon and transfer to the prepared baking sheets.

7. Repeat the above steps until you have no dough left.

TO COOK THE PASTA

1. Set a large pot of salted water on the stove to boil (see page 40). Cook the pasta in the boiling water for about 2 minutes, or until al dente. To test this, remove a piece of pasta from the pot and take a bite. It should be cooked but still slightly firm in the center.

2. When the pasta is ready, drain it through a colander and shake out the excess water.

3. Serve immediately with the sauce of your choice.

TIP: If you want to make smaller garganelli, use a clean round pencil to roll them into penne-like pasta. If your dough is not sticking, add a little water or lightly beaten egg white on the corner before rolling it.

chapter 5

RIBBON-CUT PASTA

RIBBON-CUT PASTA IS TRADITIONALLY MORE popular in Northern and Central Italy, with the region of Emilia-Romagna being the recognized center for it. In Romagna, there is a tradition of women who specialize in making this kind of pasta, both in the home and at restaurants, and there is even a special title for them: *'zdora.*

The recipes in this chapter will guide you through the most common types of ribbon pasta, and you will put into practice the rolling and cutting skills you have learned in previous chapters. You will be working mainly with egg-based dough, and the majority of the work will simply be done using your hands and a knife. From Lasagna Sheets (page 78) to Fettuccine (page 90), Maltagliati (page 80), and Tagliolini (page 102), you will learn how to cut each shape correctly, and you will soon realize that making pasta ribbons at home could not be any easier.

<< LEFT: TAGLIATELLE (PAGE 92) WITH ZUCCHINI, CHILE PEPPER, AND PARSLEY SAUCE (PAGE 190)

lasagna sheets

Lasagna sheets are the easiest pasta you can make, and the same technique is used as the base for many ribbon pasta types. To make them, you just have to roll your egg pasta dough very thin and cut it with a knife. You can use these pasta sheets to make lasagna and cannelloni—cylindrical pasta that is stuffed and usually baked like lasagna. It is the first pasta I ever made from scratch. I remember spending many a Sunday morning rolling the dough with my parents, while Ragù alla Bolognese (page 216) was bubbling away on the stove. Pure bliss! **SERVES 4**

PREP TIME: 1 HOUR | **COOK TIME:** 1 TO 2 MINUTES

EQUIPMENT

Pasta machine or rolling pin

Knife, nonserrated

3 (10-by-15-inch) baking sheets

Wide pot, to cook the pasta

Slotted spoon, to drain the pasta

Tea towel

Baking dish

INGREDIENTS

00 or all-purpose flour, for dusting

1 batch Know-by-Heart Egg Pasta Dough (page 14), rolled

Sea salt, for cooking the pasta

TO MAKE THE PASTA

1. Dust the baking sheets with 00 or all-purpose flour.

2. Roll the dough (see page 22) and feed the prepared egg pasta sheet through the machine, adjusting the settings, until setting #7. If the sheet of pasta gets too long, you can cut it in half with a knife.

3. You can do this with a rolling pin, too. Make the dough as thin and uniform as possible.

4. Using a knife, cut the dough into 6-by-4-inch sheets.

5. Transfer to the prepared baking sheets.

6. Repeat the above steps until you have no dough left.

Lasagna sheets can be served as lasagne or cannelloni. To make cannelloni, use your favorite stuffing and roll the pasta along its length. Both lasagne and cannelloni can be layered or topped with Ragù alla Bolognese (page 216), Pesto alla Genovese (page 183), or a simple Tomato and Basil Sauce (page 182). You can also use béchamel sauce, mozzarella, and grated Parmigiano-Reggiano to finish off the dish.

TO COOK THE PASTA

1. Preheat the oven to 355°F.

2. Set a wide pot full of salted water on the stove to boil (see page 40). Cook the pasta a couple of sheets at a time for 1 to 2 minutes. The pasta doesn't have to be fully cooked, as it will finish cooking in the oven. Precooking it will make it easier to layer or roll.

3. When the pasta is ready, remove it with a slotted spoon and place it on a clean tea towel until ready to use.

4. Layer your pasta in a baking dish with your favorite sauce and cheese.

5. Bake for 30 minutes.

6. Serve warm.

TIP: Cut your lasagna sheets to best suit your baking dish. This will make it easier to assemble the layers, and you will not waste any pasta.

maltagliati

 Maltagliati are a type of traditional pasta from the Emilia-Romagna region. The name literally means "poorly cut" because of their irregular shape, so don't worry about being precise when cutting them. They are among the best shapes to make when you are only just starting to make your own pasta. They can be eaten in soups, but I prefer mine with more delicate dry sauces. **SERVES 4**

PREP TIME: 1 HOUR | **COOK TIME:** 2 MINUTES

EQUIPMENT

Pasta machine or rolling pin

Knife, nonserrated

3 (10-by-15-inch) baking sheets

Large pot, to cook the pasta

Wooden spoon, to stir the pasta

Slotted spoon, to drain the pasta

INGREDIENTS

00 or all-purpose flour, for dusting

1 batch Know-by-Heart Egg Pasta Dough (page 14), rolled

Sea salt, for cooking the pasta

TO MAKE THE PASTA

1. Dust the baking sheets with 00 or all-purpose flour.

2. Roll the dough (see page 22) and feed the prepared egg pasta sheet through the machine, adjusting the settings, until setting #7. If the sheet of pasta gets too long, you can cut it in half with a knife.

3. You can do this with a rolling pin, too. Make the dough as thin and uniform as possible.

4. Using a knife, cut out your dough into 6-by-4-inch sheets.

5. Dust the pasta sheets with flour and let them rest for 5 minutes so they are not too sticky.

6. Put them one on top of the other (maximum three sheets) and, using a sharp knife, cut the pasta sheets into 1½- to 2-inch irregular shapes resembling a rhombus.

serving suggestion

Maltagliati can be served with Eggplant and Tuna Sauce (page 206), Tuna Ricotta and Olive Sauce (page 175), Sausage Sauce (page 214), or Cream Sauce with Salmon (page 191).

7. Separate the cut pasta and transfer to the prepared baking sheets.

8. Repeat the above steps until you have no dough left.

TO COOK THE PASTA

1. Set a large pot of salted water on the stove to boil (see page 40). Cook the pasta for about 2 minutes, or until al dente. To test this, remove a piece of pasta from the pot and take a bite. It should be cooked but still slightly firm in the center.

2. When the pasta is ready, remove it with a slotted spoon and gently shake out the excess water.

3. Serve immediately with the sauce of your choice.

TIP: To make maltagliati, you can also use the trimmings left over from your other pasta shapes; just make sure they are all the same thickness. There is no wasting in Italian cooking!

lasagnette

Lasagnette are the widest kind of egg pasta ribbons after lasagna sheets. In fact, the name *lasagnette* literally means "small lasagna." For their rustic appearance and texture, they are best served with tomato-based and meat sauces. **SERVES 4**

PREP TIME: 1 HOUR | **COOK TIME:** 2 MINUTES

EQUIPMENT

Pasta machine or rolling pin

Knife, nonserrated

3 (10-by-15-inch) baking sheets

Large pot, to cook the pasta

Wooden spoon, to stir the pasta

Colander, to drain the pasta

INGREDIENTS

00 or all-purpose flour, for dusting

1 batch Know-by-Heart Egg Pasta Dough (page 14), rolled

Sea salt, for cooking the pasta

TO MAKE THE PASTA

1. Dust the baking sheets with 00 or all-purpose flour.

2. Roll the dough (see page 22) and feed the prepared egg pasta sheet through the machine, adjusting the settings, until setting #7.

3. You can do this with a rolling pin too. Make the dough as thin and uniform as possible.

4. Cut the sheet of pasta into a 6- to 10-inch-long sheet and dust it with flour. Let it rest for 5 minutes.

5. Roll the sheet of pasta along its shorter edge.

6. Using a knife, cut the roll crosswise into 1½-inch-wide slices.

7. Delicately open up the sliced pasta with your hands, dust with a little flour, and make it into a loose nest.

8. Transfer to the prepared baking sheets.

9. Repeat the above steps until you have no dough left.

Lasagnette can be served with Spicy Pork Ragù (page 212), Sausage Sauce (page 214), or with a simple Tomato and Basil Sauce (page 182).

TO COOK THE PASTA

1. Set a large pot of salted water on the stove to boil (see page 40). Cook the pasta for about 2 minutes, or until al dente. To test this, remove a piece of pasta from the pot and take a bite. It should be cooked but still slightly firm in the center.

2. When the pasta is ready, drain it through a colander and shake out the excess water.

3. Serve immediately with the sauce of your choice.

TIP: Dust your lasagnette with flour before making them into a nest, or they may stick. You can also keep them flat on a baking sheet to prevent them from sticking.

sagne

 Sagne come from the Central Italian regions of Abruzzo and Molise. They are like short tagliatelle, but the dough is made with durum wheat flour and no eggs. They are the typical "poor man's food," rustic and comforting. They are traditionally added to hearty chickpea or bean soups. **SERVES 4**

PREP TIME: 1 HOUR | **COOK TIME:** 2 MINUTES

EQUIPMENT

Pasta machine or rolling pin

Knife, nonserrated

3 (10-by-15-inch) baking sheets

Large pot, to cook the pasta

Wooden spoon, to stir the pasta

Colander, to drain the pasta

INGREDIENTS

Durum wheat flour, for dusting

1 batch Know-by-Heart Durum Wheat Pasta Dough (page 16), rolled

Sea salt, for cooking the pasta

TO MAKE THE PASTA

1. Dust the baking sheets with durum wheat flour.

2. Roll the dough (see page 22) and feed the prepared egg pasta sheet through the machine, adjusting the settings, until setting #7.

3. You can do this with a rolling pin, too. Make the dough as thin and uniform as possible.

4. Cut the sheet of pasta into 2-inch-wide strips and then cut them across into ½-inch-long pieces.

5. Transfer to the prepared baking sheets.

6. Repeat the above steps until you have no dough left.

Sagne can be served in Chickpea Soup (page 204) or a simple Tomato and Basil Sauce (page 182).

TO COOK THE PASTA

1. Set a large pot of salted water on the stove to boil (see page 40). Cook the pasta for about 2 minutes, or until al dente. To test this, remove a piece of pasta from the pot and take a bite. It should be cooked but still slightly firm in the center.

2. When the pasta is ready, drain it through a colander and shake out the excess water.

3. Serve immediately with the sauce of your choice.

TIP: Sagne's dimensions make them ideal to serve with your favorite soup. Try substituting barlotti or cannellini beans for chickpeas in Chickpea Soup (page 204) for a change. You can also cook them directly in the soup if you prefer.

lagane

Lagane are like wide pappardelle, and are originally from Southern Italy. Unlike pappardelle, though, they are made with durum wheat flour and do not require the use of eggs. They are not as well known as other ribbon pastas, but they are indeed delicious. You can serve them with soups or the tomato-based sauce of your choice. **SERVES 4**

PREP TIME: 1 HOUR | **COOK TIME:** 2 MINUTES

EQUIPMENT

Pasta machine or rolling pin

Knife, nonserrated

3 (10-by-15-inch) baking sheets

Large pot, to cook the pasta

Wooden spoon, to stir the pasta

Colander, to drain the pasta

INGREDIENTS

Durum wheat flour, for dusting

1 batch Know-by-Heart Durum Wheat Pasta Dough (page 16), rolled

Sea salt, for cooking the pasta

TO MAKE THE PASTA

1. Dust the baking sheets with durum wheat flour.

2. Roll the dough (see page 22) and feed the prepared pasta sheet through the machine, adjusting the settings, until setting #7.

3. You can do this with a rolling pin too. Make the dough as thin and uniform as possible.

4. Cut the sheet of pasta into a 6- to 10-inch-long sheet and dust it with flour. Let it rest for 5 minutes.

5. Roll the sheet of pasta along its shorter edge.

6. Using a knife, cut the roll crosswise into 1-inch-wide slices.

7. Delicately open up the sliced pasta with your hands, dust with a little flour, and make it into a loose nest.

8. Transfer to the prepared baking sheets.

9. Repeat the above steps until you have no dough left.

Lagane can be served with Chickpea Soup (page 204), Ragù alla Bolognese (page 216), or Sausage Sauce (page 214).

TO COOK THE PASTA

1. Set a large pot of salted water on the stove to boil (see page 40). Cook the pasta for about 2 minutes, or until al dente. To test this, remove a piece of pasta from the pot and take a bite. It should be cooked but still slightly firm in the center.

2. When the pasta is ready, drain it through a colander and shake out the excess water.

3. Serve immediately with the sauce of your choice.

TIP: Lagane are a great vegan option for any pappardelle lover as they are just slightly wider and contain no eggs.

pappardelle

Pappardelle originate from Tuscany. It is a type of ribbon pasta similar to fettuccine, but broader. Their width can vary between ⅔ inch and ¾ inch. The name derives from the verb *pappare*, which means "to gobble up." They are considered more rustic than tagliatelle and were originally served with bold sauces made with venison, wild boar, or hare. **SERVES 4**

PREP TIME: 1 HOUR | **COOK TIME:** 2 MINUTES

EQUIPMENT

Pasta machine or rolling pin

Knife, nonserrated

3 (10-by-15-inch) baking sheets

Large pot, to cook the pasta

Wooden spoon, to stir the pasta

Colander, to drain the pasta

INGREDIENTS

00 or all-purpose flour, for dusting

1 batch Know-by-Heart Egg Pasta Dough (page 14), rolled

Sea salt, for cooking the pasta

TO MAKE THE PASTA

1. Dust the baking sheets with 00 or all-purpose flour.

2. Roll the dough (see page 22) and feed the prepared egg pasta sheet through the machine, adjusting the settings, until setting #7.

3. You can do this with a rolling pin too. Make the dough as thin and uniform as possible.

4. Cut the sheet of pasta into a 6- to 10-inch-long sheet and dust it with flour. Let it rest for 5 minutes.

5. Roll the sheet of pasta along its shorter edge.

6. Using a knife, cut the roll crosswise into ⅔-inch-wide slices.

7. Delicately open up the sliced pasta with your hands, dust with a little flour, and form it into a loose nest.

Pappardelle can be served with Creamy Mushroom Sauce (page 192), Cream Sauce with Ham and Peas (page 193), Tuna, Ricotta, and Olive Sauce (page 175), or Sausage Sauce (page 214).

8. Transfer to the prepared baking sheets.

9. Repeat the above steps until you have no dough left.

TO COOK THE PASTA

1. Set a large pot of salted water on the stove to boil (see page 40). Cook the pasta for about 2 minutes, or until al dente. To test this, remove a piece of pasta from the pot and take a bite. It should be cooked but still slightly firm in the center.

2. When the pasta is ready, drain it through a colander and shake out the excess water.

3. Serve immediately with the sauce of your choice.

TIP: Pappardelle's wider surface helps them grip the sauce better, thus making them the ideal pasta type for both bold tomato-based and more delicate creamy sauces.

fettuccine

Fettuccine are a type of ribbon pasta commonly found in Rome and other Central Italian areas. It is very similar to tagliatelle, but slightly wider in width. The name comes from the word *fettuccia*, which means "little slice," because just like tagliatelle, fettuccine are made by cutting slices of rolled egg pasta dough. **SERVES 4**

PREP TIME: 1 HOUR | **COOK TIME:** 2 MINUTES

EQUIPMENT

Pasta machine or rolling pin

Knife, nonserrated

3 (10-by-15-inch) baking sheets

Large pot, to cook the pasta

Wooden spoon, to stir the pasta

Colander, to drain the pasta

INGREDIENTS

00 or all-purpose flour, for dusting

1 batch Know-by-Heart Egg Pasta Dough (page 14), rolled

Sea salt, for cooking the pasta

TO MAKE THE PASTA

1. Dust the baking sheets with 00 or all-purpose flour.

2. Roll the dough (see page 22) and feed the prepared egg pasta sheet through the machine, adjusting the settings, until setting #7.

3. You can do this with a rolling pin too. Make the dough as thin and uniform as possible.

4. Cut the sheet of pasta into a 6- to 10-inch-long sheet and dust it with flour. Let it rest for 5 minutes.

5. Roll the sheet of pasta along its shorter edge.

6. Using a knife, cut the roll crosswise into ⅖-inch-wide slices.

7. Delicately open up the sliced pasta with your hands, dust with a little flour, and make it into a loose nest.

8. Transfer to the prepared baking sheets.

9. Repeat the above steps until you have no dough left.

Fettuccine can be served with Ragù alla Bolognese (page 216), Creamy Mushroom Sauce (page 192), Tuna, Ricotta, and Olive Sauce (page 175), Lemon Sauce (page 188), Zucchini, Chile Pepper, and Parsley Sauce (page 190), or a simple Tomato and Basil Sauce (page 182).

TO COOK THE PASTA

1. Set a large pot of salted water on the stove to boil (see page 40). Cook the pasta for about 2 minutes, or until al dente. To test this, remove a piece of pasta from the pot and take a bite. It should be cooked but still slightly firm in the center.

2. When the pasta is ready, drain it through a colander and shake out the excess water.

3. Serve immediately with the sauce of your choice.

TIP: There is no need to be precise with your measurements. Just remember to cut fettuccine slightly wider than tagliatelle.

tagliatelle

Tagliatelle are one of the most famous types of handmade pasta, and they originate from the city of Bologna, in Central Italy. The same area is also known for tortellini, lasagne, and Ragù alla Bolognese (page 216), the sauce tagliatelle is traditionally served with. The name tagliatelle comes from the verb *tagliare*, which means "to cut," as the sheets of dough are cut into ribbons to make tagliatelle. They are extremely versatile and go well with many sauces. SERVES 4

PREP TIME: 1 HOUR | **COOK TIME:** 2 MINUTES

EQUIPMENT

Pasta machine or rolling pin

Knife, nonserrated

3 (10-by-15-inch) baking sheets

Large pot, to cook the pasta

Wooden spoon, to stir the pasta

Colander, to drain the pasta

INGREDIENTS

00 or all-purpose flour, for dusting

1 batch Know-by-Heart Egg Pasta Dough (page 14), rolled

Sea salt, for cooking the pasta

TO MAKE THE PASTA

1. Dust the baking sheets with 00 or all-purpose flour.

2. Roll the dough (see page 22) and feed the prepared egg pasta sheet through the machine, adjusting the settings, until setting #7.

3. You can do this with a rolling pin too. Make the dough as thin and uniform as possible.

4. Cut the sheet of pasta into a 6- to 10-inch-long sheet and dust it with flour. Let it rest for 5 minutes.

5. Roll the sheet of pasta along its shorter edge.

6. Using a knife, cut the roll crosswise into ¼-inch-wide slices.

7. Delicately open up the sliced pasta with your hands, dust with a little flour, and make it into a loose nest.

serving suggestion

For an authentic Italian experience, serve tagliatelle with Ragù alla Bolognese (page 216). It is the first sauce Italians associate with tagliatelle, since they are both traditional dishes from Bologna. However, tagliatelle are also great served with Zucchini, Chile Pepper, and Parsley Sauce (page 190); Artichoke Sauce (page 197); Tuna, Ricotta, and Olive Sauce (page 175); Lemon Sauce (page 188); or a simple Tomato and Basil Sauce (page 182).

8. Transfer to the prepared baking sheets.

9. Repeat the above steps until you have no dough left.

TO COOK THE PASTA

1. Set a large pot of salted water on the stove to boil (see page 40). Cook the pasta for about 2 minutes, or until al dente. To test this, remove a piece of pasta from the pot and take a bite. It should be cooked but still slightly firm in the center.

2. When the pasta is ready, drain it through a colander and shake out the excess water.

3. Serve immediately with the sauce of your choice.

TIP: If you want to cook your tagliatelle immediately, cover them with a clean tea towel while waiting for the water to boil to prevent a crust from forming on the surface.

quadrucci

Quadrucci are a small egg pasta shape that is traditionally served in broth. As the name suggests—the term comes from the word *quadrato*, which means "square"—they are little squares of pasta. I suggest making only a half batch of the egg pasta dough for this recipe. You usually need about half the normal pasta amount when you are serving quadrucci in broth. **SERVES 4**

PREP TIME: 1 HOUR | **COOK TIME:** 1 MINUTE

EQUIPMENT

Pasta machine or rolling pin

Knife, nonserrated

3 (10-by-15-inch) baking sheets

Large pot, to cook the pasta

Wooden spoon, to stir the pasta

INGREDIENTS

00 or all-purpose flour, for dusting

½ batch Know-by-Heart Egg Pasta Dough (page 14), rolled

Sea salt, for cooking the pasta

Broth, for cooking the pasta

TO MAKE THE PASTA

1. Dust the baking sheets with 00 or all-purpose flour.

2. Roll the dough (see page 22) and feed the prepared egg pasta sheet through the machine, adjusting the settings, until setting #7. If the sheet of pasta gets too long, you can cut it in half with a knife.

3. You can do this with a rolling pin too. Make the dough as thin and uniform as possible.

4. Using a knife, cut out 6-by-4-inch sheets of pasta.

5. Dust the pasta sheets with flour and let them rest for 5 minutes so they are not too sticky.

6. Put them one on top of the other (maximum 3 sheets) and, using a sharp knife, cut the sheets into ⅓-inch strips and then cut these strips into ⅓-inch squares.

serving suggestion

Quadrucci are usually served in broth. Cook them directly in Italian Chicken Broth (page 201).

7. Separate the cut pasta and transfer to the prepared baking sheets.

8. Repeat the above steps until you have no dough left.

TO COOK THE PASTA

1. Set a large pot of Italian Chicken Broth (page 201) on the stove to boil and cook the pasta for no more than 1 minute, or until al dente. To test this, remove a piece of pasta from the pot and take a bite. It should be cooked but still slightly firm in the center.

2. Season with salt.

3. When the pasta is ready, serve it with the broth.

TIP: Make sure to shake off any excess flour that might cling to the quadrucci, so as not to cloud the broth. For a vegetarian option, use vegetable broth.

rombi

Rombi are similar to maltagliati in shape, but they are much more regular in size and they have crinkled edges. This pasta is best eaten with seafood-based sauces. I remember eating perfect-looking rombi at a restaurant in Sicily. They were made with a swordfish sauce and tasted so good that I wish I could go back in time to enjoy that dish again. **SERVES 4**

PREP TIME: 1 HOUR | **COOK TIME:** 2 MINUTES

EQUIPMENT

Pasta machine or rolling pin

Crinkle-edge pastry wheel

3 (10-by-15-inch) baking sheets

Wide pot, to cook the pasta

Wooden spoon, to stir the pasta

Colander, to drain the pasta

INGREDIENTS

00 or all-purpose flour, for dusting

1 batch Know-by-Heart Egg Pasta Dough (page 14), rolled

Sea salt, for cooking the pasta

TO MAKE THE PASTA

1. Dust the baking sheets with 00 or all-purpose flour.

2. Roll the dough (see page 22) and feed the prepared egg pasta sheet through the machine, adjusting the settings, until setting #7. If the sheet of pasta gets too long, you can cut it in half with a knife.

3. You can do this with a rolling pin too. Make the dough as thin and uniform as possible.

4. Using a crinkle-edge pastry wheel, cut out 6-by-4-inch sheets of pasta.

5. Dust the pasta sheets with flour and let them rest for 5 minutes so they are not too sticky.

6. Put them one on top of the other (maximum 3 sheets) and, using a crinkle-edge pastry wheel, cut the pasta sheets into 1½- to 2-inch diamond shapes.

Rombi can be served with Eggplant and Tuna Sauce (page 206), Prawn and Zucchini Sauce (page 187), or Cream Sauce with Salmon (page 191).

7. Separate the cut pasta and transfer to the prepared baking sheets.

8. Repeat the above steps until you have no dough left.

TO COOK THE PASTA

1. Set a large pot of salted water on the stove to boil (see page 40). Cook the pasta for about 2 minutes, or until al dente. To test this, remove a piece of pasta from the pot and take a bite. It should be cooked but still slightly firm in the center.

2. When the pasta is ready, drain it through a colander and shake out the excess water.

3. Serve immediately with the sauce of your choice.

TIP: To make rombi more easily, cut the pasta sheets in half along the longer side and then cut again diagonally at a 45-degree angle across the sheets to make diamond shapes.

mafalde

Mafalde—also known as *manfredi* or *reginette*—are a type of durum wheat ribbon pasta characterized by their long, wide rectangular shape and crinkled edges. They are similar to pappardelle in width, but while pappardelle are most commonly found in Tuscany, mafalde are typical of Naples, where they are served with bold meat sauces and ragù. They are named in honor of Princess Mafalda of Savoy, one of the last Italian princesses. **SERVES 4**

PREP TIME: 1 HOUR | **COOK TIME:** 2 MINUTES

EQUIPMENT

Pasta machine or rolling pin

Crinkle-edge pastry wheel

3 (10-by-5-inch) baking sheets

Large pot, to cook the pasta

Wooden spoon, to stir the pasta

Colander, to drain the pasta

INGREDIENTS

Durum wheat flour, for dusting

1 batch Know-by-Heart Durum Wheat Pasta Dough (page 16), rolled

Sea salt, for cooking the pasta

TO MAKE THE PASTA

1. Dust the baking sheets with durum wheat flour.

2. Roll the dough (see page 22) and feed the prepared pasta sheet through the machine, adjusting the settings, until setting #7.

3. You can do this with a rolling pin too. Make the dough as thin and uniform as possible.

4. Cut the sheet of pasta into a 6- to 10-inch-long sheet and dust it with flour. Let it rest for 5 minutes.

5. Using a crinkle edge pastry wheel, slice it into ⅖-inch-wide slices.

6. Delicately pick up the sliced pasta with your hands, dust with a little flour, and make it into a loose nest.

7. Transfer to the prepared baking sheets.

8. Repeat the above steps until you have no dough left.

Mafalde can be served with Spicy Pork Ragù (page 212), Pumpkin and Sausage Sauce (page 208), or Sausage Sauce (page 214).

TO COOK THE PASTA

1. Set a large pot of salted water on the stove to boil (see page 40). Cook the pasta for about 2 minutes, or until al dente. To test this, remove a piece of pasta from the pot and take a bite. It should be cooked but still slightly firm in the center.

2. When the pasta is ready, drain it through a colander and shake out the excess water.

3. Serve immediately with the sauce of your choice.

TIP: Mafalde can also be made using the egg dough pasta recipe, even though they are traditionally made with durum wheat dough, like the majority of the pasta from Southern Italy. They can be paired with the same sauces above.

trenette

Trenette are a type of narrow, flat pasta traditionally made in Genoa and the region of Liguria. They are wider than taglierini, but about half the width of tagliatelle. They are traditionally paired with Pesto alla Genovese (page 183), especially when made with the addition of boiled potatoes and green beans. **SERVES 4**

PREP TIME: 1 HOUR | **COOK TIME:** 1 MINUTE

EQUIPMENT

Pasta machine or rolling pin

Knife, nonserrated

3 (10-by-15-inch) baking sheets

Large pot, to cook the pasta

Wooden spoon, to stir the pasta

Colander, to drain the pasta

INGREDIENTS

00 or all-purpose flour, for dusting

1 batch Know-by-Heart Egg Pasta Dough (page 14), rolled

Sea salt, for cooking the pasta

TO MAKE THE PASTA

1. Dust the baking sheets with 00 or all-purpose flour.

2. Roll the dough (see page 22) and feed the prepared egg pasta sheet through the machine, adjusting the settings, until setting #7.

3. You can do this with a rolling pin too. Make the dough as thin and uniform as possible.

4. Cut the sheet of pasta into a 6- to 10-inch-long sheet and dust it with flour. Let it rest for 5 minutes.

5. Roll the sheet of pasta along its shorter edge.

6. Using a knife, cut the roll crosswise into ⅛-inch-wide slices.

7. Delicately open up the sliced pasta with your hands, dust with a little flour, and make it into a loose nest.

8. Transfer to the prepared baking sheets.

9. Repeat the above steps until you have no dough left.

Trenette are traditionally served with Pesto alla Genovese (page 183) or Walnut Sauce (page 179), as both sauces are from Genoa. However, they can also be paired with Aglio, Olio, e Peperoncino Sauce (page 177); Cacio e Pepe Sauce (page 180); or Prawn and Zucchini Sauce (page 187).

TO COOK THE PASTA

1. Set a large pot of salted water on the stove to boil (see page 40). Cook the pasta for about 1 minute, or until al dente. To test this, remove a piece of pasta from the pot and take a bite. It should be cooked but still slightly firm in the center.

2. When the pasta is ready, drain it through a colander and shake out the excess water.

3. Serve immediately with the sauce of your choice.

TIP: If serving trenette with either Pesto alla Genovese (page 183) or Walnut Sauce (page 179), mix them with the sauce of your choice in a serving bowl and not in the pot. This will prevent the sauces from cooking and oxidizing.

tagliolini

Tagliolini are mostly common in the regions of Molise and Piedmont, where they are known as *tajarin*. They are similar to flat spaghetti and are only ⅛ inch wide. They are usually paired with light and delicate sauces made with either vegetables or seafood, or a mix of both. **SERVES 4**

PREP TIME: 1 HOUR | **COOK TIME:** 1 MINUTE

EQUIPMENT

Pasta machine or rolling pin

Knife, nonserrated

3 (10-by-15-inch) baking sheets

Large pot, to cook the pasta

Wooden spoon, to stir the pasta

Colander, to drain the pasta

INGREDIENTS

00 or all-purpose flour, for dusting

1 batch Know-by-Heart Egg Pasta Dough (page 14), rolled

Sea salt, for cooking the pasta

TO MAKE THE PASTA

1. Dust the baking sheets with 00 or all-purpose flour.

2. Roll the dough (see page 22) and feed the prepared egg pasta sheet through the machine, adjusting the settings, until setting #7.

3. You can do this with a rolling pin too. Make the dough as thin and uniform as possible.

4. Cut the sheet of pasta into a 6- to 10-inch-long sheet and dust it with flour. Let it rest for 5 minutes.

5. Roll the sheet of pasta along its shorter edge.

6. Using a knife, cut the roll crosswise into ⅛-inch-wide slices.

7. Delicately open up the sliced pasta with your hands, dust with a little flour, and make it into a loose nest.

8. Transfer to the prepared baking sheets.

9. Repeat the above steps until you have no dough left.

Tagliolini can be served with Artichoke Sauce (page 197); Lemon Sauce (page 188); Cream Sauce with Salmon (page 191); Aglio, Olio, e Peperoncino Sauce (page 177); Cacio e Pepe Sauce (page 180); or Prawn and Zucchini Sauce (page 187).

TO COOK THE PASTA

1. Set a large pot of salted water on the stove to boil (see page 40). Cook the pasta for about 1 minute, or until al dente. To test this, remove a piece of pasta from the pot and take a bite. It should be cooked but still slightly firm in the center.

2. When the pasta is ready, quickly drain it through a colander.

3. Serve immediately with the sauce of your choice.

TIP: Tagliolini are a little tricky to cook, because of their very thin surface. To prepare them perfectly and avoid them from sticking, don't drain the tagliolini completely before adding them to the pot with your chosen sauce.

stringozzi

Stringozzi (or *strangozzi*) are an Italian pasta made from durum wheat flour traditionally made in the Central region of Umbria. In shape, they are something in between tagliolini and spaghetti alla chitarra, but they are strictly made by hand and are very rustic in appearance. The name of the pasta is drawn from its resemblance to shoelaces, which are called *stringhe* in Italian. SERVES 4

PREP TIME: 1 HOUR | **COOK TIME:** 2 TO 3 MINUTES

EQUIPMENT

Pasta machine or rolling pin

Knife, nonserrated

3 (10-by-15-inch) baking sheets

Large pot, to cook the pasta

Wooden spoon, to stir the pasta

Colander, to drain the pasta

INGREDIENTS

Durum wheat flour, for dusting

1 batch Know-by-Heart Durum Wheat Pasta Dough (page 16), rolled

Sea salt, for cooking the pasta

TO MAKE THE PASTA

1. Dust the baking sheets with durum wheat flour.

2. Roll the dough (see page 22) and feed the prepared egg pasta sheet through the machine, adjusting the settings, until setting #5 or #6.

3. You can do this with a rolling pin, too. The dough has to be a little thicker than the one for tagliatelle, but still uniform.

4. Cut the sheet of pasta into a 6- to 10-inch-long sheet and dust it with flour. Let it rest for 5 minutes.

5. Roll the sheet of pasta along its shorter edge.

6. Using a knife, cut the roll crosswise into $\frac{1}{10}$-inch-wide slices.

7. Delicately open up the sliced pasta with your hands, dust with a little flour, and make it into a loose nest.

serving suggestion

Stringozzi can be served with Artichoke Sauce (page 197); Sausage Sauce (page 214); Aglio, Olio e Peperoncino Sauce (page 177); Zucchini, Chile Pepper, and Parsley Sauce (page 190); Bucaiola Sauce (page 178); Cacio e Pepe Sauce (page 180); or Aglione Sauce (page 194).

8. Transfer to the prepared baking sheets.

9. Repeat the above steps until you have no dough left.

TO COOK THE PASTA

1. Set a large pot of salted water on the stove to boil (see page 40). Cook the pasta for 2 to 3 minutes, or until al dente. To test this, remove a piece of pasta from the pot and take a bite. It should be cooked but still slightly firm in the center.

2. When the pasta is ready, drain it through a colander and shake out the excess water.

3. Serve immediately with the sauce of your choice.

TIP: No need to be very precise with your measurements when making stringozzi. It is a very rustic kind of pasta, and the exact dimensions vary from town to town and family to family.

spaghetti alla chitarra

Spaghetti alla chitarra—also known as *troccoli* or *tonnarelli*—are a kind of pasta typical of Central and Southern Italy, Apulia in particular. They have a square cross-section about ⅒-inch thick and a porous texture that allows the sauce to grip well. They are slightly narrower but thicker than tagliolini, and they look like square spaghetti. Traditionally, they are made using a specific tool called a *chitarra* (meaning guitar)—a wooden frame with a series of parallel wires crossing it. I am lucky enough to have one, which was given to me by my aunt Stella, who lives in Apulia. If you don't have one, you can make this pasta using a sharp, nonserrated knife. **SERVES 4**

PREP TIME: 1 HOUR | **COOK TIME:** 3 TO 4 MINUTES

EQUIPMENT

Rolling pin

Knife, nonserrated, or chitarra

3 (10-by-15-inch) baking sheets

Large pot, to cook the pasta

Wooden spoon, to stir the pasta

Colander, to drain the pasta

INGREDIENTS

Durum wheat flour, for dusting

1 batch Know-by-Heart Durum Wheat Pasta Dough (page 16)

Sea salt, for cooking the pasta

TO MAKE THE PASTA

1. Dust the baking sheets with durum wheat flour.

2. With a rolling pin (see page 22), roll the dough into an 8-by-5-inch, ⅒-inch-thick rectangular sheet. Dust it with flour.

3. If you have a chitarra, place the sheet of dough on its strings and, using the rolling pin, roll and push the dough through the strings so that it gets cut into spaghetti.

4. If you don't have a chitarra, dust the sheet of pasta with a little flour and let it rest for 5 minutes. Then roll it along its shorter edge. Use a sharp, nonserrated knife to slice it into ⅒-inch-wide slices, just as you would do for tagliolini.

serving suggestion

Spaghetti alla Chitarra are usually served with Spicy Pork Ragù (page 212); Sausage Sauce (page 214); Bucaiola Sauce (page 178); Aglio, Olio, e Peperoncino Sauce (page 177); Zucchini, Chile Pepper, and Parsley Sauce (page 190); Cacio e Pepe Sauce (page 180); or a simple Tomato and Basil Sauce (page 182).

5. Delicately open up the sliced pasta with your hands, dust with a little flour, and make it into a loose nest.

6. Transfer to the prepared baking sheets.

7. Repeat the above steps until you have no dough left.

TO COOK THE PASTA

1. Set a large pot of salted water on the stove to boil (see page 40). Cook the pasta for 3 to 4 minutes, or until *al dente*. To test this, remove a piece of pasta from the pot and take a bite. It should be cooked but still slightly firm in the center.

2. When the pasta is ready, drain it through a colander and shake out the excess water.

3. Serve immediately with the sauce of your choice.

TIP: Spaghetti alla Chitarra can also be made using the egg pasta dough in this book; however, they will take longer to cook and the dough may be a bit harder to roll. If you are just starting out, I suggest trying the durum wheat version first.

chapter 6
STUFFED PASTA

S TUFFED PASTA IS the kind of pasta I enjoy making the most. You can play around with different stuffing ingredients, flavors, and shapes, so you can turn your final dish into something new every time.

Making stuffed pasta at home does require a little more time than pasta ribbons. You need to make the stuffing and fill each piece with care so that it doesn't open up when you cook it. However, your efforts will be repaid and your taste buds will thank you when you finally get to eat it.

In this chapter I will guide you through some of the best stuffed pasta recipes. If serving stuffed pasta in broth, I suggest making only half a batch. If required, you can dry and freeze the extra pasta (see page 38). Each pasta shape is presented with a specific filling, but feel free to mix and match.

The recipes have been ordered from the easiest to the hardest, so that you can practice and develop your skills as you go along.

<< LEFT: MOZZARELLA, BASIL, AND PARMIGIANO-REGGIANO RAVIOLI (PAGE 110)

mozzarella, basil, and parmigiano-reggiano ravioli

Ravioli are possibly the most famous kind of stuffed pasta. This shape is common throughout Italy, where you can find it in local cuisines with different stuffing. In the Northern city of Mantua, for example, ravioli—known locally as tortelli—are filled with pumpkin, while in Sardinia, ravioli are filled with lemon and ricotta. I like to stuff mine with this very Mediterranean filling made with fresh mozzarella, basil, and Parmigiano-Reggiano. SERVES 4 TO 6

PREP TIME: 1 HOUR AND 15 MINUTES | **COOK TIME:** 2 MINUTES

EQUIPMENT

Food processor

Colander

Fork

Pasta machine or rolling pin

Crinkle-edge pastry wheel or pizza cutter

3 (10-by-15-inch) baking sheets

Plastic wrap, to keep the dough covered

Wooden spoon, to stir the pasta

Large pot, to cook the pasta

Slotted spoon, to drain the pasta

INGREDIENTS
FOR THE STUFFING

1½ pounds fresh mozzarella, roughly chopped

¼ cup basil leaves

¾ cup finely grated Parmigiano-Reggiano

Sea salt

Freshly ground black pepper

FOR THE PASTA

00 or all-purpose flour, for dusting

1 batch Know-by-Heart Egg Pasta Dough (page 14), rolled

Sea salt, for cooking the pasta

TO MAKE THE STUFFING

1. In a food processor, roughly blend the fresh mozzarella and basil leaves. Transfer to a colander and let sit for 30 minutes to drain.

2. Transfer the mixture to a bowl, add the Parmigiano-Reggiano, and mix well with a fork. Season with sea salt and freshly ground black pepper.

TO MAKE THE PASTA

1. Dust the baking sheets with 00 or all-purpose flour.

2. Roll the dough (see page 22) and feed the prepared egg pasta sheet through the machine, adjusting the settings, until setting #8. If the sheet of pasta gets too long, you can cut it in half with a knife.

3. You can do this with a rolling pin, too. Make the dough as thin and uniform as possible.

4. Dust your work surface with flour and put your rolled dough on it.

5. Make hazelnut-sized balls with the stuffing and put them on the lower half of the sheet of pasta. Make sure to leave enough space in between the balls, so you can close your pasta well and cut it.

6. Wet the sides of the dough with a little water to help the pasta stick.

7. Fold the other half of the sheet onto the filling and press well all around. Make sure not to leave any air bubbles inside, or the pasta will open while cooking and the filling will come out.

8. Using a crinkle-edge pastry wheel or a pizza cutter, cut around the filling in a squarish shape and remove the excess dough.

9. Transfer to the prepared baking sheets.

10. Repeat the above steps until you have no dough left.

continued >

serving suggestion

Mozzarella, Basil, and Parmigiano-Reggiano Ravioli can be served with Butter and Sage Sauce (page 174) or a simple Tomato and Basil Sauce (page 182).

TO COOK THE PASTA

1. Set a large pot of salted water on the stove to boil (see page 40). Cook the pasta for about 2 minutes, or until al dente. To test this, remove a piece of pasta from the pot and take a bite. It should be cooked but still slightly firm in the center.

2. When the pasta is ready, remove with a slotted spoon and gently shake out the excess water.

3. Serve immediately with the sauce of your choice.

TIP: Use only fresh mozzarella for this recipe and not the harder shredded kind. You can also use buffalo mozzarella. Always make sure your stuffing is not too wet. If it is, add a little extra Parmigiano-Reggiano to thicken it.

spinach and ricotta ravioli tondi

 Ravioli tondi are round-looking ravioli made with egg pasta dough. If made small (about 1½ inches) and filled with meat-based stuffings, they are also known as *anolini*. I prefer bigger ravioli tondi as they can be filled with a wider variety of stuffings, like a classic yet sophisticated spinach and ricotta filling, which is also called *di magro*—a.k.a. meatless. SERVES 4 TO 6

PREP TIME: 1 HOUR AND 30 MINUTES | **COOK TIME:** 2 MINUTES

EQUIPMENT

Pot, to wilt the spinach

Knife, nonserrated

Cutting board

Bowl

Fork

Pasta machine or rolling pin

2½-inch round pasta cutter or pizza cutter

3 (10-by-15-inch) baking sheets

Plastic wrap, to keep the dough covered

Wooden spoon, to stir the pasta

Large pot, to cook the pasta

Slotted spoon, to drain the pasta

INGREDIENTS
FOR THE STUFFING

1⅓ pounds raw spinach

1⅓ cups ricotta

⅔ cup finely grated Parmigiano-Reggiano

2 large eggs

Pinch ground nutmeg

Sea salt

Freshly ground black pepper

FOR THE PASTA

00 or all-purpose flour, for dusting

1 batch Know-by-Heart Egg Pasta Dough (page 14), rolled

Sea salt, for cooking the pasta

continued >

TO MAKE THE STUFFING

1. Trim and wash the spinach. Place the spinach leaves, still wet from washing, into a pot. Add ⅓ cup of water and put the pot over medium heat. Cook for 2 to 3 minutes, until the spinach is wilted. Drain well and squeeze all the water out.

2. Cut the cooked spinach very finely with a knife and put it in a bowl with the ricotta, Parmigiano-Reggiano, eggs, and nutmeg. Mix well using a fork.

3. Season with sea salt and freshly ground black pepper.

TO MAKE THE PASTA

1. Dust the baking sheets with 00 or all-purpose flour.

2. Roll the dough (see page 22) and feed the prepared egg pasta sheet through the machine, adjusting the settings, until setting #8. If the sheet of pasta gets too long, you can cut it in half with a knife.

3. You can do this with a rolling pin, too. Make the dough as thin and uniform as possible.

4. Dust your work surface with flour and put your rolled dough on it.

5. With a round pasta cutter, cut out 2½-inch rounds of pasta.

6. Put 1 teaspoon of filling on half of the pasta rounds, lightly wet the edges with a little water, and top with the other half of the pasta rounds. Use a fork to press well to seal.

7. Transfer to the prepared baking sheets.

8. Repeat the above steps until you have no dough left.

Spinach and Ricotta Ravioli Tondi can be served with Butter and Sage Sauce (page 174), a simple Tomato and Basil Sauce (page 182), Cacio e Pepe Sauce (page 180) or in Italian Chicken Broth (page 201)—in this case you can cook your ravioli directly in the broth.

TO COOK THE PASTA

1. Set a large pot of salted water on the stove to boil (see page 40). Cook the pasta for about 2 minutes, or until al dente. To test this, remove a piece of pasta from the pot and take a bite. It should be cooked but still slightly firm in the center.

2. When the pasta is ready, remove with a slotted spoon and gently shake out the excess water.

3. Serve immediately with the sauce of your choice.

TIP: If you want to serve Spinach and Ricotta Ravioli Tondi in chicken broth, I suggest you make them smaller—about 1 to 1½ inches—so they can easily fit into the spoon while eating.

smoked salmon and ricotta mezzelune

Mezzelune, which literally means "half-moons," are a kind of ravioli with curved edges. Made with egg pasta dough, mezzelune pair well with a variety of stuffings, especially ricotta-based ones. The combination I like the most is smoked salmon and ricotta: creamy, delicate, and slightly smoky. This is one of my favorite stuffed pastas to make, as it doesn't take a long time to shape and it always comes out looking perfect. **SERVES 4 TO 6**

PREP TIME: 1 HOUR | **COOK TIME:** 2 MINUTES

EQUIPMENT

Food processor

Bowl

Fork

Pasta machine or rolling pin

2½-inch round pasta cutter or pizza cutter

3 (10-by-15-inch) baking sheets

Plastic wrap, to keep the dough covered

Wooden spoon, to stir the pasta

Large pot, to cook the pasta

Slotted spoon, to drain the pasta

INGREDIENTS
FOR THE STUFFING

1 pound ricotta cheese

½ pound smoked salmon, roughly chopped

2 tablespoons chives, chopped

Sea salt

FOR THE PASTA

00 or all-purpose flour, for dusting

1 batch Know-by-Heart Egg Pasta Dough (page 14), rolled

Sea salt, for cooking the pasta

serving suggestion

Smoked Salmon and Ricotta Mezzelune can be served with Butter and Sage Sauce (page 174), Lemon Sauce (page 188), or a simple Tomato and Basil Sauce (page 182).

TO MAKE THE STUFFING

In a food processor, blend the ricotta and smoked salmon until creamy. Transfer to a bowl, add the chives, and mix well with a fork. Season with salt.

TO MAKE THE PASTA

1. Dust the baking sheets with 00 or all-purpose flour.

2. Roll the dough (see page 22) and feed the prepared egg pasta sheet through the machine, adjusting the settings, until setting #8. If the sheet of pasta gets too long, you can cut it in half with a knife.

3. You can do this with a rolling pin, too. Make the dough as thin and uniform as possible.

4. Dust your work surface with flour and put your rolled dough on it.

5. Make hazelnut-sized balls about ⅔ of an inch with the stuffing and put them on the lower half of the sheet of pasta. Make sure to leave enough space in between, so you can close your pasta well and cut the semicircular shapes.

6. Wet the sides of the dough with a little water to help the pasta stick.

7. Fold the other half of the sheet onto the filling and press well all around. Make sure not to leave any air bubbles inside, or the pasta will open while cooking and the filling will come out.

8. Using a 2½-inch round cutter or a pizza cutter, cut the pasta in a semicircular shape.

9. Remove the excess dough and transfer to the prepared baking sheets.

10. Repeat the above steps until you have no dough left.

TO COOK THE PASTA

1. Set a large pot of salted water on the stove to boil (see page 40). Cook the pasta for about 2 minutes, or until al dente. To test this, remove a piece of pasta from the pot and take a bite. It should be cooked but still slightly firm in the center.

2. When the pasta is ready, remove with a slotted spoon and gently shake out the excess water.

3. Serve immediately with the sauce of your choice.

TIP: If you want, you can also use a glass or a small bowl to cut out the mezzelune. This way, you can make them as big or as small as you like.

cacio e pepe triangolini

Triangolini, as the name suggests, are triangle-shaped ravioli made with egg pasta dough and a variety of stuffings. I like to fill mine with *cacio e pepe*, which means "cheese and pepper"—a classic combination. Usually served as a pasta sauce, here it has been transformed into a stuffing, with a little bit of creativity. I prefer to serve these triangolini with a light Butter and Sage Sauce (page 174) to let the filling shine. **SERVES 4 TO 6**

PREP TIME: 1 HOUR AND 20 MINUTES | **COOK TIME:** 2 MINUTES

EQUIPMENT

Bowl

Fork

Pasta machine or rolling pin

Crinkle-edge pastry wheel or pizza cutter

3 (10-by-15-inch) baking sheets

Plastic wrap, to keep the dough covered

Wooden spoon, to stir the pasta

Large pot, to cook the pasta

Slotted spoon, to drain the pasta

INGREDIENTS
FOR THE STUFFING

3 cups Pecorino Romano, finely grated

14 ounces cream cheese

Milk, if required

Sea salt

⅓ tablespoon freshly ground black pepper

FOR THE PASTA

00 or all-purpose flour, for dusting

1 batch Know-by-Heart Egg Pasta Dough (page 14), rolled

Sea salt, for cooking the pasta

serving suggestion

Cacio e Pepe Triangolini can be served with Butter and Sage Sauce (page 174) or a simple Tomato and Basil Sauce (page 182).

TO MAKE THE STUFFING

Using a fork, mix the Pecorino Romano and cream cheese together in a bowl until creamy. Add a little milk, if required, to soften the mixture. Season with sea salt and freshly ground black pepper.

TO MAKE THE PASTA

1. Dust the baking sheets with 00 or all-purpose flour.

2. Roll the dough (see page 22) and feed the prepared egg pasta sheet through the machine, adjusting the settings, until setting #8. If the sheet of pasta gets too long, you can cut it in half with a knife.

3. You can do this with a rolling pin, too. Make the dough as thin and uniform as possible.

4. Dust your work surface with flour and put your rolled dough on it.

5. Using a crinkle-edge pastry wheel, cut out 2½-inch squares of pasta.

6. Put 1 teaspoon of filling on each square of pasta, lightly wet the corners with a little water, and close it in half to make a triangle shape. Press well to seal.

7. Transfer to the prepared baking sheets.

8. Do this for all the squares, then roll out some more pasta dough and continue until you have no dough left.

TO COOK THE PASTA

1. Set a large pot of salted water on the stove to boil (see page 40). Cook the pasta for about 2 minutes, or until al dente. To test this, remove a piece of pasta from the pot and take a bite. It should be cooked but still slightly firm in the center.

2. When the pasta is ready, remove with a slotted spoon and gently shake out the excess water.

3. Serve immediately with the sauce of your choice.

TIP: You can use a fork to press down the edges when sealing triangolini, especially if you are not using a crinkle-edge pastry wheel to cut out the pasta squares. This will make your pasta look better.

pumpkin ravioloni quadrati

Ravioloni quadrati are square-looking ravioli made with egg pasta dough. They are much bigger than regular ravioli and are never served in broth. They can be filled with many soft stuffings. This delicate pumpkin filling goes extremely well with this pasta shape. **SERVES 4 TO 6**

PREP TIME: 2 HOURS, PLUS 2 HOURS RESTING TIME FOR THE STUFFING |
COOK TIME: 2 MINUTES

EQUIPMENT

Baking sheet, to bake the pumpkin

Bowl

Fork

Potato masher

3 (10-by-15-inch) baking sheets

Pasta machine or rolling pin

Crinkle-edge pastry wheel or pizza cutter

Plastic wrap, to keep the dough covered

Wooden spoon, to stir the pasta

Large pot, to cook the pasta

Slotted spoon, to drain the pasta

INGREDIENTS
FOR THE STUFFING

2 pounds peeled and seeded pumpkin, cut into slices about 2 inches thick

3 tablespoons extra-virgin olive oil

1½ cups finely grated Parmigiano-Reggiano

Pinch ground nutmeg

Sea salt

Breadcrumbs, if required

FOR THE PASTA

00 or all-purpose flour, for dusting

1 batch Know-by-Heart Egg Pasta Dough (page 14), rolled

Sea salt, for cooking the pasta

TO MAKE THE STUFFING

1. Brush the pumpkin with the oil and bake it in a preheated oven at 350°F until tender. When ready, mash the pumpkin. Let it cool down completely and transfer to a bowl.

2. Add the grated Parmigiano-Reggiano, nutmeg, and sea salt, and mix with a fork. If the stuffing doesn't hold its shape, add some breadcrumbs to it until you can make it into soft balls.

3. Refrigerate for 2 hours before using.

TO MAKE THE PASTA

1. Dust the baking sheets with 00 or all-purpose flour.

2. Roll the dough (see page 22) and feed the prepared egg pasta sheet through the machine, adjusting the settings, until setting #8. If the sheet of pasta gets too long, you can cut it in half with a knife.

3. You can do this with a rolling pin, too. Make the dough as thin and uniform as possible.

4. Roll 2 sheets of pasta.

5. Dust your work surface with flour and put one of your rolled sheets on it.

6. Make 2-inch balls with the stuffing and put them on the sheet of pasta. Make sure to leave some space in between, so you can close your pasta well.

7. Wet the sides of the dough around the stuffing with a little water to help the pasta stick.

8. Top with the other sheet of pasta and press well all around. Make sure not to leave any air bubbles inside, or the pasta will open while cooking and the filling will come out.

9. Using a crinkle-edge pastry wheel or a pizza cutter, cut around the filling into 3½-inch squares, and remove the excess dough.

10. Use a fork to press the edges well to seal.

11. Transfer to the prepared baking sheets.

12. Repeat the above steps until you have no dough left.

continued >

Pumpkin Ravioloni Quadrati can be served with Butter and Sage Sauce (page 174), Pumpkin and Sausage Sauce (page 208), or Lemon Sauce (page 188).

TO COOK THE PASTA

1. Set a large pot of salted water on the stove to boil (see page 40). Cook the pasta for about 2 minutes, or until al dente. To test this, remove a piece of pasta from the pot and take a bite. It should be cooked but still slightly firm in the center.

2. When the pasta is ready, remove with a slotted spoon and gently shake out the excess water.

3. Serve immediately with the sauce of your choice.

TIPS: For better presentation results, serve Pumpkin Ravioloni Quadrati on a flat plate instead of in a pasta bowl. Given their size, you can't serve many per person, and you want them to shine on the plate.

goat's cheese and chive cuori

Cuori are a kind of heart-shaped ravioli made with egg pasta dough and a variety of stuffings. The name, appropriately, means "hearts" in Italian. This shape is not traditional, and it came about in more recent years as a different way to shape ravioli. I like to fill mine with goat's cheese and chives, a simple stuffing with bold flavors. **SERVES 4 TO 6**

PREP TIME: 1 HOUR AND 20 MINUTES | **COOK TIME:** 2 MINUTES

EQUIPMENT

Bowl

Fork

3 (10-by-15-inch) baking sheets

Pasta machine or rolling pin

Heart-shaped cookie cutter

Plastic wrap, to keep the dough covered

Wooden spoon, to stir the pasta

Large pot, to cook the pasta

Slotted spoon, to drain the pasta

INGREDIENTS
FOR THE STUFFING

⅔ pound soft goat's cheese

14 ounces mascarpone

1½ cups finely grated Parmigiano-Reggiano

3 tablespoons chopped chives

Sea salt

FOR THE PASTA

00 or all-purpose flour, for dusting

1 batch Know-by-Heart Egg Pasta Dough (page 14), rolled

Sea salt, for cooking the pasta

continued >

serving suggestion

Goat's Cheese and Chive Cuori can be served with Butter and Sage Sauce (page 174), Lemon Sauce (page 188), or a simple Tomato and Basil Sauce (page 182).

TO MAKE THE STUFFING

Using a fork, mix the goat's cheese, mascarpone, Parmigiano-Reggiano, and chopped chives in a bowl until creamy and well combined. Season with sea salt.

TO MAKE THE PASTA

1. Dust the baking sheets with 00 or all-purpose flour.

2. Roll the dough (see page 22) and feed the prepared egg pasta sheet through the machine, adjusting the settings, until setting #8. If the sheet of pasta gets too long, you can cut it in half with a knife.

3. You can do this with a rolling pin, too. Make the dough as thin and uniform as possible.

4. Dust your work surface with flour and put your rolled dough on it.

5. Using a heart-shaped cookie cutter, cut out the pasta.

6. Put ½ teaspoon of filling on half of the pasta hearts, lightly wet the edges with a little water, and top with the remaining pasta hearts. Use a fork to press the edges well to seal.

7. Transfer to the prepared baking sheets.

8. Repeat the above steps until you have no dough left.

TO COOK THE PASTA

1. Set a large pot of salted water on the stove to boil (see page 40). Cook the pasta for about 2 minutes, or until al dente. To test this, remove a piece of pasta from the pot and take a bite. It should be cooked but still slightly firm in the center.

2. When the pasta is ready, remove with a slotted spoon and gently shake out the excess water.

3. Serve immediately with the sauce of your choice.

TIP: This is the perfect kind of pasta to serve to that special someone in your life. They are a Valentine's Day favorite. They are also very popular with kids!

lemon and ricotta stelle

Stelle are a nontraditional kind of star-shaped ravioli made with egg pasta dough and a variety of stuffings. They are called *stelle* as the word means "stars" in Italian. It's a fun shape and you need only a cookie cutter to make it. I usually fill my stelle with lemon and ricotta, but any soft stuffing will work well. **SERVES 4 TO 6**

PREP TIME: 1 HOUR AND 20 MINUTES | **COOK TIME:** 2 MINUTES

EQUIPMENT

Bowl

Fork

Pasta machine or rolling pin

Star-shaped cookie cutter

3 (10-by-15-inch) baking sheets

Plastic wrap, to keep the dough covered

Wooden spoon, to stir the pasta

Large pot, to cook the pasta

Slotted spoon, to drain the pasta

INGREDIENTS
FOR THE STUFFING

1 pound ricotta cheese

Grated zest of 2 big lemons

2 cups finely grated Parmigiano-Reggiano

Milk, if required

Sea salt

FOR THE PASTA

00 or all-purpose flour, for dusting

1 batch Know-by-Heart Egg Pasta Dough (page 14), rolled

Sea salt, for cooking the pasta

continued >

serving suggestion

Lemon and Ricotta Stelle can be served with Butter and Sage Sauce (page 174), Lemon Sauce (page 188), or a simple Tomato and Basil Sauce (page 182).

TO MAKE THE STUFFING

Using a fork, mix the ricotta and lemon zest together in a bowl until creamy. Add the Parmigiano-Reggiano and mix well. You may have to add some milk to the mixture to make it softer, depending on how dry the ricotta is. Season with sea salt.

TO MAKE THE PASTA

1. Dust the baking sheets with 00 or all-purpose flour.

2. Roll the dough (see page 22) and feed the prepared egg pasta sheet through the machine, adjusting the settings, until setting #8. If the sheet of pasta gets too long, you can cut it in half with a knife.

3. You can do this with a rolling pin, too. Make the dough as thin and uniform as possible.

4. Dust your work surface with flour and put your rolled dough on it.

5. Using a star-shaped cookie cutter, cut out the pasta.

6. Put ½ teaspoon of filling on half of the pasta stars, lightly wet the edges with a little water, and top with the remaining pasta stars. Use your fingers to press well to seal.

7. Transfer to the prepared baking sheets.

8. Repeat the above steps until you have no dough left.

TO COOK THE PASTA

1. Set a large pot of salted water on the stove to boil (see page 40). Cook the pasta for about 2 minutes, or until al dente. To test this, remove a piece of pasta from the pot and take a bite. It should be cooked but still slightly firm in the center.

2. When the pasta is ready, remove with a slotted spoon and gently shake out the excess water.

3. Serve immediately with the sauce of your choice.

TIP: This is the perfect kind of pasta to serve during the winter holidays. The kids will love it!

prawn and leek caramelle

 Caramelle are a more recent shape of stuffed pasta made with egg pasta dough. Resembling wrapped candies, caramelle are really popular among children, and the best part is they are very easy to make, so you can involve the kids in the shaping process. I like to fill caramelle with a chunky yet delicate prawn and leek stuffing. **SERVES 4 TO 6**

PREP TIME: 1 HOUR AND 40 MINUTES | **COOK TIME:** 3 TO 4 MINUTES

EQUIPMENT

Cutting board

Knife, nonserrated

Skillet, to cook the stuffing

Bowl

Fork

Pasta machine or rolling pin

Crinkle-edge pastry wheel or pizza cutter

3 (10-by-15-inch) baking sheets

Plastic wrap, to keep the dough covered

Wooden spoon, to stir the pasta

Large pot, to cook the pasta

Slotted spoon, to drain the pasta

INGREDIENTS
FOR THE STUFFING

2 tablespoons extra-virgin olive oil

1 leek, finely sliced

1 pound peeled and deveined prawns, chopped

Sea salt

Freshly ground black pepper

¼ cup breadcrumbs, plus additional if needed

FOR THE PASTA

00 or all-purpose flour, for dusting

1 batch Know-by-Heart Egg Pasta Dough (page 14), rolled

Sea salt, for cooking the pasta

continued >

serving suggestion

Prawn and Leek Caramelle can be served with Butter and Sage Sauce (page 174), Lemon Sauce (page 188), or a simple Tomato and Basil Sauce (page 182).

TO MAKE THE STUFFING

1. Heat the olive oil in the skillet over medium-low heat. Add the leek and sauté for 2 to 3 minutes, or until the leek is tender. Add the prawns and sauté for a couple of minutes. Mix well. Make sure the mixture is as dry as possible. Season with sea salt and freshly ground black pepper. Transfer to a bowl and let cool completely.

2. Add enough breadcrumbs to bring the ingredients together and make the stuffing as dry as possible. Mix well with a fork.

TO MAKE THE PASTA

1. Dust the baking sheets with 00 or all-purpose flour.

2. Roll the dough (see page 22) and feed the prepared egg pasta sheet through the machine, adjusting the settings, until setting #8. If the sheet of pasta gets too long, you can cut it in half with a knife.

3. You can do this with a rolling pin too. Make the dough as thin and uniform as possible.

4. Dust your work surface with flour and put your rolled dough on it.

5. With a crinkle-edge pastry wheel or a pizza cutter, cut out 3-by-4-inch rectangles of pasta.

6. Put about 1½ teaspoons of filling in the center of each rectangle, and lightly wet the edges with a little water.

7. Roll the pasta along its longer side, then twist the edges as if you were wrapping a candy.

8. Transfer to the prepared baking sheets.

9. Repeat the above steps until you have no dough left.

TO COOK THE PASTA

1. Set a large pot of salted water on the stove to boil (see page 40). Cook the pasta for 3 to 4 minutes, or until al dente. To test this, remove a piece of pasta from the pot and take a bite. It should be cooked but still slightly firm in the center.

2. When the pasta is ready, remove with a slotted spoon and gently shake out the excess water.

3. Serve immediately with the sauce of your choice.

TIP: Make sure to taste caramelle before removing them from the heat, as the pasta is folded on itself and may require a little extra cooking time.

parmigiano-reggiano fagottini

Fagottini are a more modern kind of stuffed pasta made using egg pasta dough and a variety of stuffings, but my favorite version is made with a simple Parmigiano-Reggiano filling. They also vary in size and can be served either in chicken broth or with other pasta sauces. Fagottini's shape resembles little parcels, just as the name suggests. In fact, *fagottini* is the Italian term for "little bags." **SERVES 4 TO 6**

PREP TIME: 1 HOUR AND 40 MINUTES | **COOK TIME:** 3 MINUTES

EQUIPMENT

Bowl

Fork

Pasta machine or rolling pin

Crinkle-edge pastry wheel or pizza cutter

3 (10-by-15-inch) baking sheets

Plastic wrap, to keep the dough covered

Wooden spoon, to stir the pasta

Large pot, to cook the pasta

Slotted spoon, to drain the pasta

INGREDIENTS
FOR THE STUFFING

3 cups finely grated Parmigiano-Reggiano

2 large eggs

Pinch ground nutmeg

Sea salt

FOR THE PASTA

00 or all-purpose flour, for dusting

1 batch Know-by-Heart Egg Pasta Dough (page 14), rolled

1 large egg, lightly beaten

Sea salt, for cooking the pasta

continued >

serving suggestion

Parmigiano-Reggiano Fagottini can be served with Butter and Sage Sauce (page 174), with a simple Tomato and Basil Sauce (page 182), or in Italian Chicken Broth (page 201)—in this case you can cook fagottini directly in the broth.

TO MAKE THE STUFFING

Using a fork, mix the finely grated Parmigiano-Reggiano, eggs, and nutmeg in a bowl. Season with sea salt.

TO MAKE THE PASTA

1. Dust the baking sheets with 00 or all-purpose flour.

2. Roll the dough (see page 22) and feed the prepared egg pasta sheet through the machine, adjusting the settings, until setting #8. If the sheet of pasta gets too long, you can cut it in half with a knife.

3. You can do this with a rolling pin, too. Make the dough as thin and uniform as possible.

4. Dust your work surface with flour and put your rolled dough on it.

5. Cut out 1½-inch squares (for soup fagottini) or 2½-inch squares (for any other sauce). Brush them with some lightly beaten egg.

6. Put ¼ scant teaspoon of filling on each small square of pasta and ½ scant teaspoon of filling on each big square of pasta. Close it by folding and joining the sides together toward the center, making a little parcel. Press well to seal.

7. Transfer to the prepared baking sheets.

8. Do this for all the squares, then roll out some more pasta dough and continue until you have no dough left.

TO COOK THE PASTA

1. Set a large pot of salted water on the stove to boil (see page 40). Cook the pasta for about 3 minutes, or until al dente. To test this, remove a piece of pasta from the pot and take a bite. It should be cooked but still slightly firm in the center.

2. When the pasta is ready, remove with a slotted spoon and gently shake out the excess water.

3. Serve immediately with the sauce of your choice.

TIP: Use a beaten egg to brush the pasta squares to help seal fagottini properly and ensure they do not open up while cooking.

casoncelli alla bergamasca

This is the traditional stuffed pasta from the Northern Italian city of Bergamo, not far from Milan. Bergamo is a very ancient city that dates back to the Celtic times. Casoncelli (or *casonsèi* as they are called in the local dialect) have a very particular shape. They are traditionally stuffed with inexpensive local ingredients, such as sausage, bread-crumbs, parsley, eggs, and garlic. In modern times, cheese and a few other "noble" ingredients were added, turning a simple dish into a delightful meal. **SERVES 4 TO 6**

PREP TIME: 1 HOUR AND 20 MINUTES | **COOK TIME:** 2 TO 3 MINUTES

EQUIPMENT

Food processor

Bowl

Fork

Pasta machine or rolling pin

2½-inch round pasta cutter or pizza cutter

3 (10-by-15-inch) baking sheets

Plastic wrap, to keep the dough covered

Wooden spoon, to stir the pasta

Large pot, to cook the pasta

Slotted spoon, to drain the pasta

INGREDIENTS
FOR THE STUFFING

12 ounces Italian pork sausage, casing removed, chopped

6 ounces mortadella

2 garlic cloves

1 large egg

3 tablespoons chopped flat-leaf parsley

1½ cups breadcrumbs

5 tablespoons milk

¾ cup finely grated Parmigiano-Reggiano

Sea salt

FOR THE PASTA

00 or all-purpose flour, for dusting

1 batch Know-by-Heart Egg Pasta Dough (page 14), rolled

Sea salt, for cooking the pasta

continued >

TO MAKE THE STUFFING

1. In a food processor, combine the sausage, mortadella, garlic, egg, and parsley, and process until combined. Add the breadcrumbs and process again to combine.

2. Transfer the meat mixture to a bowl, stir in the milk and grated Parmigiano-Reggiano, and mix with a fork. Season with sea salt.

TO MAKE THE PASTA

1. Dust the baking sheets with 00 or all-purpose flour.

2. Roll the dough (see page 22) and feed the prepared egg pasta sheet through the machine, adjusting the settings, until setting #8. If the sheet of pasta gets too long, you can cut it in half with a knife.

3. You can do this with a rolling pin, too. Make the dough as thin and uniform as possible.

4. Dust your work surface with flour and put your rolled dough on it.

5. Make small balls with the stuffing (about the size of a hazelnut) and put them on the lower half of the sheet of pasta. Make sure to leave some space in between, so you can close your pasta well.

6. Wet the sides of the dough with a little water to help the pasta stick.

7. Fold the other half of the sheet onto the filling and press well all around. Make sure not to leave any air bubbles inside, or the pasta will open while cooking and the filling will come out.

8. Using a 2½-inch round cutter or a pizza cutter, cut the pasta in a semicircular shape, just as if you were making mezzelune.

9. Put the mezzaluna standing on the round side. Put your index finger in the center of the mezzaluna and carefully press down. Pinch the sides and gently push them towards the center to shape casoncelli.

10. Transfer to the prepared baking sheets.

11. Repeat the above steps until you have no dough left.

Casoncelli alla Bergamasca can be served with Butter and Sage Sauce (page 174), Bucaiola Sauce (page 178), or a simple Tomato and Basil Sauce (page 182).

TO COOK THE PASTA

1. Set a large pot of salted water on the stove to boil (see page 40). Cook the pasta for 2 to 3 minutes, or until al dente. To test this, remove a piece of pasta from the pot and take a bite. It should be cooked but still slightly firm in the center.

2. When the pasta is ready, remove with a slotted spoon and gently shake out the excess water.

3. Serve immediately with the sauce of your choice.

TIP: Use only pure pork sausages for best results. When making casoncelli, use a sausage that doesn't contain fennel seeds, which are too strong in flavor and would not work well in this stuffing.

cappelletti romagnoli

Cappelletti are a kind of pasta stuffed with meat, cheese, or vegetables and folded so as to resemble small, peaked hats—the word *cappelletti* literally means "little hats." Cappelletti come from the Emilia-Romagna region, and they can be made small to be eaten in chicken broth or slightly bigger to be eaten with other sauces. The traditional recipe calls for capon in the stuffing, but turkey or chicken work just as well. **SERVES 4 TO 6**

PREP TIME: 2 HOURS AND 15 MINUTES | **COOK TIME:** 4 TO 5 MINUTES

EQUIPMENT

Skillet, to cook the meat

Knife, nonserrated

Cutting board

Bowl

Pasta machine or rolling pin

1½- or 2½-inch round pasta cutter or pizza cutter

3 (10-by-15-inch) baking sheets

Plastic wrap, to keep the dough covered

Wooden spoon, to stir the pasta

Large pot, to cook the pasta

Slotted spoon, to drain the pasta

INGREDIENTS
FOR THE STUFFING

2 tablespoons unsalted butter

7 ounces turkey or chicken breast, roughly chopped

8 ounces ricotta

1 cup finely grated Parmigiano-Reggiano

1 large egg plus 1 large egg yolk

Finely grated zest of ½ lemon (optional)

Pinch ground nutmeg

Sea salt

Freshly ground black pepper

FOR THE PASTA

00 or all-purpose flour, for dusting

1 batch Know-by-Heart Egg Pasta Dough (page 14)

Sea salt, for cooking the pasta

TO MAKE THE STUFFING

1. Heat the butter in a skillet over medium-high heat until melted. Add the turkey or chicken breast and sauté until cooked through, about 5 minutes. Remove from the heat, season with salt, and let cool.

2. Cut the cooked meat as finely as you can with a sharp knife and transfer it to a bowl.

3. Add the ricotta, finely grated Parmigiano-Reggiano, egg, egg yolk, lemon zest, and nutmeg, and mix by hand. Season with sea salt and pepper.

TO MAKE THE PASTA

1. Dust the baking sheets with 00 or all-purpose flour.

2. Roll the dough (see page 22) and feed the prepared egg pasta sheet through the machine, adjusting the settings, until setting #8. If the sheet of pasta gets too long, you can cut it in half with a knife.

3. You can do this with a rolling pin too. Make the dough as thin and uniform as possible.

4. Dust your work surface with flour and put your rolled dough on it.

5. With a round pasta cutter, cut out 1½-inch rounds of pasta (for soup cappelletti) or 2½-inch rounds of pasta (for any other sauce).

6. Put a scant ¼ teaspoon of filling on each small round of pasta or a scant ½ teaspoon of filling on each big round of pasta. Lightly wet the corners with a little water, and close the round in half to make a half-moon shape.

7. Pick up the half-moon shape and hold it at the corners with two hands. Bring the two opposite corners together and press to seal them. The rounded edge will flip up a little to give the pasta its characteristic shape.

8. Transfer to the prepared baking sheets.

9. Do this for all the pasta rounds, then roll out some more pasta dough and continue until you have no dough left.

continued >

serving suggestion

Cappelletti Romagnoli can be served with Ragù alla Bolognese (page 216), Butter and Sage Sauce (page 174), a simple Tomato and Basil Sauce (page 182) or in Italian Chicken Broth (page 201)—in this case you can cook cappelletti directly in the broth.

TO COOK THE PASTA

1. Set a large pot of salted water on the stove to boil (see page 40). Cook the pasta for 4 to 5 minutes, or until al dente. To test this, remove a piece of pasta from the pot and take a bite. It should be cooked but still slightly firm in the center.

2. When the pasta is ready, remove with a slotted spoon and gently shake out the excess water.

3. Serve immediately with the sauce of your choice.

TIP: The lemon zest in this recipe is optional. In fact, not all traditional recipes call for it, but I like the hint of freshness that it adds to the stuffing.

potato, sausage, and mushroom cappellacci

 Cappellacci are much bigger than cappelletti, and while cappelletti are usually filled with meat and served in broth, cappellacci can be stuffed with softer fillings, like this delightful potato, sausage, and mushroom stuffing. The term *cappellaccio* means "big old hat," and this stuffed pasta is yet another traditional dish from the Emilia-Romagna region. **SERVES 4 TO 6**

PREP TIME: 2 HOURS AND 15 MINUTES | **COOK TIME:** 4 TO 5 MINUTES

EQUIPMENT

Skillet, to cook the stuffing

Food processor

Bowl

Pasta machine or rolling pin

5-inch round pasta cutter or pizza cutter

3 (10-by-15-inch) baking sheets

Plastic wrap, to keep the dough covered

Wooden spoon, to stir the pasta

Large pot, to cook the pasta

Slotted spoon, to drain the pasta

INGREDIENTS
FOR THE STUFFING

3 tablespoons extra-virgin olive oil

2 garlic cloves, halved

⅔ pound mushrooms (fresh porcini, chanterelles, or cremini work best), cleaned and sliced

¾ pound Italian pork sausage, casing removed, chopped

⅓ cup white wine

Sea salt

2 tablespoons chopped flat-leaf parsley

1 pound potatoes, boiled and roughly chopped

1 cup finely grated Parmigiano-Reggiano

FOR THE PASTA

00 or all-purpose flour, for dusting

1 batch Know-by-Heart Egg Pasta Dough (page 14)

Sea salt, for cooking the pasta

continued >

TO MAKE THE STUFFING

1. Heat the olive oil in a skillet over medium-high heat. Add the garlic and sauté for about a minute. Add the sliced mushrooms and mix well. Add the chopped sausage and sauté until brown.

2. Add the white wine and season with sea salt. As soon as the alcohol from the wine evaporates, add the chopped parsley and remove the pan from the heat.

3. Put this mixture into a food processor, add the boiled potatoes, and blend roughly.

4. Transfer to a bowl, add the finely grated Parmigiano-Reggiano, and mix with a fork. Adjust the salt if required. Let cool down completely.

TO MAKE THE PASTA

1. Dust the baking sheets with 00 or all-purpose flour.

2. Roll the dough (see page 22) and feed the prepared egg pasta sheet through the machine, adjusting the settings, until setting #8. If the sheet of pasta gets too long, you can cut it in half with a knife.

3. You can do this with a rolling pin too. Make the dough as thin and uniform as possible.

4. Dust your work surface with flour and put your rolled dough on it.

5. With a round pasta cutter, cut out 5-inch rounds of pasta.

6. Put about 1 tablespoon of filling on each round of pasta, lightly wet the corners with a little water, and close the round in half to make a half-moon shape.

7. Pick up the half-moon shape and hold it at the corners with two hands. Bring the two opposite corners together and press to seal them. The rounded edge will flip up a little to give the pasta its characteristic shape.

8. Transfer to the prepared baking sheets.

9. Do this for all the pasta rounds, then roll out some more pasta dough and continue until you have no dough left.

Potato, Sausage, and Mushroom Cappellacci can be served with Butter and Sage Sauce (page 174), Bucalola Sauce (page 178), or a simple Tomato and Basil Sauce (page 182).

TO COOK THE PASTA

1. Set a large pot of salted water on the stove to boil (see page 40). Cook the pasta for 4 to 5 minutes, or until al dente. To test this, remove a piece of pasta from the pot and take a bite. It should be cooked but still slightly firm in the center.

2. When the pasta is ready, remove with a slotted spoon and gently shake out the excess water.

3. Serve immediately with the sauce of your choice.

TIP: Serve only 4 or 5 cappellacci per person as they are very big. Make sure to keep the dough covered with plastic wrap at all times while not working with it to prevent it from drying out.

tortellini bolognesi

 Tortellini are a kind of stuffed pasta originally from the Emilia-Romagna region. The Modena and Bologna versions are particularly famous, and they both use a similar stuffing made of pork meat, prosciutto, mortadella, and Parmigiano-Reggiano—all local products. They can also be filled with a simple Parmigiano-Reggiano stuffing (page 129) for a vegetarian option. Tortellini's shape resembles a navel, so they are also known as "Venus' navel." **SERVES 4 TO 6**

PREP TIME: 2 HOURS | **COOK TIME:** 4 TO 5 MINUTES

EQUIPMENT

Food processor

Medium bowl

Pasta machine or rolling pin

Crinkle-edge pastry wheel or pizza cutter

3 (10-by-15-inch) baking sheets

Plastic wrap, to keep the dough covered

Wooden spoon, to stir the pasta

Large pot, to cook the pasta

Slotted spoon, to drain the pasta

INGREDIENTS
FOR THE STUFFING

6 ounces pork loin, chopped into small pieces

3½ ounces mortadella

3½ ounces Italian prosciutto (preferably Prosciutto di Parma)

1 cup finely grated Parmigiano-Reggiano

2 large eggs

Pinch ground nutmeg

Sea salt

FOR THE PASTA

00 or all-purpose flour, for dusting

1 batch Know-by-Heart Egg Pasta Dough (page 14)

Sea salt, for cooking the pasta

TO MAKE THE STUFFING

1. In a food processor, blend together the pork loin, mortadella, and prosciutto until combined.

2. In a medium bowl, combine the meat mixture with the grated Parmigiano-Reggiano, eggs, and nutmeg, and mix by hand.

3. Season with sea salt.

TO MAKE THE PASTA

1. Dust the baking sheets with 00 or all-purpose flour.

2. Roll the dough (see page 22) and feed the prepared egg pasta sheet through the machine, adjusting the settings, until setting #8. If the sheet of pasta gets too long, you can cut it in half.

3. You can do this with a rolling pin, too. Make the dough as thin and uniform as possible.

4. Dust your work surface with flour and put your rolled dough on it.

5. With a crinkle-edge pastry wheel or pizza cutter, cut out 1½-inch squares (for soup tortellini) or 2½-inch squares (for any other sauce).

6. Put a scant ¼ teaspoon of filling on each small square of pasta and a scant ½ teaspoon of filling on each big square of pasta. Lightly wet the corners with a little water, and close the square in half to make a triangle.

7. Bring the two opposite corners together by wrapping them around your index finger, and press the bottom edges together to seal them. The remaining corner will flip up a little, too, giving the tortellino its characteristic shape.

8. Transfer to the prepared baking sheets.

9. Do this for all the squares, then roll out some more pasta dough and continue until you have no dough left.

continued >

Tortellini Bolognesi are traditionally served with Ragù alla Bolognese (page 216), since they are both dishes from Bologna. However, they can also be served with Butter and Sage Sauce (page 174), with a simple Tomato and Basil Sauce (page 182), or in Italian Chicken Broth (page 201)—in this case you can cook tortellini directly in the broth.

TO COOK THE PASTA

1. Set a large pot of salted water on the stove to boil (see page 40). Cook the pasta for 4 to 5 minutes, or until al dente. To test this, remove a piece of pasta from the pot and take a bite. It should be cooked but still slightly firm in the center.

2. When the pasta is ready, remove with a slotted spoon and gently shake out the excess water.

3. Serve immediately with the sauce of your choice.

TIP: Roll out only a little piece of dough at a time as the pasta dries up very fast, which will make shaping tortellini really hard. Keep the dough covered with plastic wrap at all times—even the ready-to-fill squares—unless you are working with it.

walnut and gorgonzola tortelloni

Tortelloni are a much bigger version of tortellini. While tortellini are traditionally filled with a meat-based stuffing, tortelloni are best filled with a softer stuffing, as you will need to cut them to eat them. My favorite tortelloni stuffing is walnut and Gorgonzola: rich and creamy, but with some crunch. This is a very easy stuffing that can be prepared in 5 minutes. **SERVES 4 TO 6**

PREP TIME: 1 HOUR AND 40 MINUTES | **COOK TIME:** 4 TO 5 MINUTES

EQUIPMENT

Medium bowl

Fork

Pasta machine or rolling pin

Crinkle-edge pastry wheel or pizza cutter

3 (10-by-15-inch) baking sheets

Plastic wrap, to keep the dough covered

Wooden spoon, to stir the pasta

Large pot, to cook the pasta

Slotted spoon, to drain the pasta

INGREDIENTS
FOR THE STUFFING

1 pound Gorgonzola

9 ounces mascarpone

1½ cups finely grated Parmigiano-Reggiano

½ cup chopped walnuts

Sea salt

FOR THE PASTA

00 or all-purpose flour, for dusting

1 batch Know-by-Heart Egg Pasta Dough (page 14)

Sea salt, for cooking the pasta

continued >>

serving suggestion

Walnut and Gorgonzola Tortelloni can be served with Butter and Sage Sauce (page 174) or Walnut Sauce (page 179).

TO MAKE THE STUFFING

In a medium mixing bowl, stir the Gorgonzola, mascarpone, Parmigiano-Reggiano, and walnuts together with a fork until well combined. Season with salt.

TO MAKE THE PASTA

1. Dust the baking sheets with 00 or all-purpose flour.

2. Roll the dough (see page 22) and feed the prepared egg pasta sheet through the machine, adjusting the settings, until setting #8. If the sheet of pasta gets too long, you can cut it in half with a knife.

3. You can do this with a rolling pin too. Make the dough as thin and uniform as possible.

4. Dust your work surface with flour and put your rolled dough on it.

5. With a crinkle edge pastry wheel or pizza cutter, cut out 4-inch squares.

6. Put about ¾ tablespoon of filling on each square of pasta, lightly wet the corners with a little water, and close the square in half to make a triangle.

7. Bring the two opposite corners together by wrapping them around your index and middle fingers, and press the bottom edges together to seal them. The remaining corner will flip up a little, too, giving the tortellone its characteristic shape.

8. Transfer to the prepared baking sheets.

9. Do this for all the squares, then roll out some more pasta dough and continue until you have no dough left.

TO COOK THE PASTA

1. Set a large pot of salted water on the stove to boil (see page 40). Cook the pasta for 4 to 5 minutes, or until al dente. To test this, remove a piece of pasta from the pot and take a bite. It should be cooked but still slightly firm in the center.

2. When the pasta is ready, remove with a slotted spoon and gently shake out the excess water.

3. Serve immediately with the sauce of your choice.

TIP: Serve only 5 or 6 tortelloni per person as they are very big and quite filling. Sprinkle them with some finely grated Parmigiano-Reggiano for extra flavor.

culurgiones all'ogliastrina

 Culurgiones all'Ogliastrina are traditional Sardinian stuffed dough pockets. *Culurgiones* means "little bundles," which accurately describes these parcels of joy. *Ogliastrina* comes from Ogliastra, the Eastern area of Sardinia where this stuffed pasta originates. Their shape resembles an ear of wheat, as Sardinia is an agricultural area. Traditionally they are made using durum wheat dough, and they are filled with a stuffing made of potatoes and Pecorino. Culurgiones are probably the most difficult pasta shape in this book, but as you make more culurgiones, you will find the process a lot easier. All it takes is a little practice. **SERVES 4 TO 6**

PREP TIME: 2 HOURS, PLUS 16 HOURS FOR INFUSING THE OIL AND RESTING THE STUFFING | **COOK TIME:** 3 MINUTES

EQUIPMENT

Small cup

Bowl

Fork

3 (10-by-15-inch) baking sheets

Pasta machine or rolling pin

3-inch round pasta cutter

Plastic wrap, to keep the dough covered

Wooden spoon, to stir the pasta

Large pot, to cook the pasta

Slotted spoon, to drain the pasta

INGREDIENTS
FOR THE STUFFING

¼ cup plus 1 tablespoon extra-virgin olive oil

2 garlic cloves, halved

1½ pounds russet potatoes, boiled and mashed

15 mint leaves, finely chopped

2 cups finely grated Pecorino Romano

Sea salt

FOR THE PASTA

Durum wheat flour, for dusting

1 batch Know-by-Heart Durum Wheat Pasta Dough (page 16)

Sea salt, for cooking the pasta

continued >

TO MAKE THE STUFFING

1. In the morning, put the garlic in the olive oil in a small cup. Cover and set aside, so that the garlic infuses the oil.

2. In the evening, mix the mashed potatoes, mint, and Pecorino Romano together. Discard the garlic and add the garlic-infused oil to the potato mixture. Season with sea salt.

3. Refrigerate for 8 hours or overnight, so that the filling thickens a bit.

TO MAKE THE PASTA

1. Dust the baking sheets with durum wheat flour.

2. Roll the dough (see page 22) and feed the pasta sheet through the machine as you would egg pasta, adjusting the settings, until setting #7. If the sheet of pasta gets too long, you can cut it in half with a knife.

3. You can do this with a rolling pin, too. The dough has to be quite thin and uniform.

4. Dust your work surface with flour and put your rolled dough on it.

5. With a round pasta cutter, cut out 3-inch rounds of pasta.

6. Place 1 scant tablespoon of filling in the middle of each circle.

7. Place the circle between your thumb and index finger. Fold the pasta around the filling so it looks like a taco. Pinch one end of the "taco" (about a ⅓-inch pinch) and fold it over one side of the seam and pinch again. Then take that pinch and fold it over the other side of the seam, overlapping the first, so that the seam resembles a braid. Continue pinching toward alternating sides until you reach the other end of the pasta taco. When you reach the end, pinch the final piece to ensure that no filling escapes.

8. Transfer to the prepared baking sheets.

9. Repeat the above steps until you have no dough left.

serving suggestion

Culurgiones all'Ogliastrina are usually served with a simple Tomato and Basil Sauce (page 182), which complements the potato and Pecorino stuffing very well. You can also serve them with Butter and Sage Sauce (page 174) or Arrabbiata Sauce (page 195).

TO COOK THE PASTA

1. Set a large pot of salted water on the stove to boil (see page 40). Cook the pasta for about 3 minutes, or until al dente. To test this, remove a piece of pasta from the pot and take a bite. It should be cooked but still slightly firm in the center.

2. When the pasta is ready, remove with a slotted spoon and gently shake out the excess water.

3. Serve immediately with the sauce of your choice.

TIP: To make the dough a little more pliable, you can add 1 to 2 tablespoons of extra-virgin olive oil to the basic durum wheat dough recipe. This will make shaping the culurgiones a little easier.

chapter 7

GNOCCHI & GNUDI

G NOCCHI ARE PROBABLY the most common kind of homemade pasta in Italy. There is no region that doesn't have a particular gnocchi recipe. In fact, they are so popular that "*Giovedì, gnocchi*"—on Thursdays, we eat gnocchi—is a very common saying in Italy. The reason is that Italy is historically a Catholic country, and people used to eat light meals or even fast on Fridays, which would make them feast and eat more on Thursdays! However, no matter when you eat them, gnocchi are still a scrumptious treat!

Even though the most famous gnocchi are made from potatoes, you can make them out of a huge variety of ingredients: broccoli, chestnut flour, butternut squash, pumpkin, semolina, and even bread! Gnocchi can be made with very little flour, and these are called *gnudi*, and are much softer than regular gnocchi, since they are mainly made of ricotta and spinach.

<< LEFT: PUMPKIN GNOCCHI (PAGE 162) WITH BUTTER AND SAGE SAUCE (PAGE 174)

ricotta gnocchi

I love the soft, silky texture and cheesy flavor of ricotta gnocchi. I discovered them only a few years ago, but they have become a family favorite. They are also quicker to make than regular potato gnocchi, as you do not need to boil potatoes to make the dough. I also find this specific dough more forgiving, so this is a good recipe to start with if you are just learning to make gnocchi. SERVES 4

PREP TIME: 50 MINUTES | **COOK TIME:** 1 TO 2 MINUTES

EQUIPMENT

Stand mixer (optional)

Gnocchi board (optional)

Large bowl

Knife, nonserrated

3 (10-by-15-inch) baking sheets

Wooden spoon, to stir the gnocchi

Large pot, to cook the gnocchi

Slotted spoon, to drain the gnocchi

INGREDIENTS

1½ cups all-purpose flour, plus more for dusting (you may require a little more or a little less depending on how moist the ricotta is)

1¼ cups ricotta cheese, set in a colander to drain for about 2 hours

1 large egg

¾ cup finely grated Parmigiano-Reggiano

1 teaspoon sea salt, plus more for cooking the gnocchi

TO MAKE THE GNOCCHI

1. Dust the baking sheets with all-purpose flour.

2. Put the ricotta, egg, Parmigiano-Reggiano, and sea salt in a large bowl.

3. Slowly add the flour and start kneading. You may have to add a little more flour. The dough is ready when it doesn't stick to your hands, but is still soft and pliable.

4. To save time, you can do this with a stand mixer. Put all the ingredients together in the bowl of the mixer fitted with the paddle attachment and knead until combined. If the dough is sticky, add a little more flour and knead by hand until it becomes smooth and pliable. The dough is ready when it doesn't stick to your hands.

5. Divide the dough into 8 to 10 balls. Roll each ball of dough into a ⅔-inch-thick rope using your fingertips.

Ricotta Gnocchi are best eaten with Butter and Sage Sauce (page 174), Gorgon-zola Sauce (page 189), Walnut Sauce (page 179), or Cream Sauce with Ham and Peas (page 193). All of these sauces complement the subtle, cheesy flavor of Ricotta Gnocchi.

6. Cut the ropes of dough into 1-inch pieces and place them on the prepared baking sheets. If you want, you can give gnocchi their traditional shape by rolling them on the tines of a fork (or on the gnocchi board) while pressing down with your thumb.

7. Repeat the above steps until you have no dough left.

8. Let the gnocchi rest for 15 minutes before cooking them.

TO COOK THE GNOCCHI

1. Set a large pot of salted water on the stove to boil (see page 40) and cook the gnocchi in the boiling water, just as you would cook pasta.

2. The gnocchi are ready as soon as they start to float. This will take 1 to 2 minutes.

3. Remove the gnocchi from the water with a slotted spoon.

4. Depending on the sauce you choose for serving, you can either sauté the gnocchi in the pot with the sauce for a minute or two, or put the gnocchi in a large serving bowl and toss them with the sauce.

5. Serve immediately.

TIP: For a more exotic flavor and a brighter color, add ¾ teaspoon of saffron powder to your dough. Simply mix it in with your grated cheese and knead the dough as you normally would.

potato gnocchi

Potato gnocchi are probably the most well-known type of gnocchi outside of Italy. Their popularity is well deserved, as they are indeed an amazing dish. If not made properly, though, they can become very dense, and there is nothing worse than chewy gnocchi! I learned how to make potato gnocchi from my Nonna Bice. Hers was the best: light, smooth, and fluffy. Don't be intimidated by the task—making gnocchi at home is very easy and they taste so much better than the gnocchi you buy in the supermarket! **SERVES 4**

PREP TIME: 1 HOUR AND 15 MINUTES | **COOK TIME:** 1 TO 2 MINUTES

EQUIPMENT

Stand mixer (optional)

Gnocchi board (optional)

Potato ricer

Knife, nonserrated

3 (10-by-15-inch) baking sheets

Wooden spoon, to stir the gnocchi

Large pot, to cook the gnocchi

Slotted spoon, to drain the gnocchi

INGREDIENTS

1 cup all-purpose flour, plus more for dusting (you may require a little more or a little less depending on the potatoes)

2¼ pounds russet potatoes, with skin on, halved

¾ teaspoon sea salt, plus more for cooking the gnocchi

1 large egg

TO MAKE THE GNOCCHI

1. Dust the baking sheets with all-purpose flour.

2. To cook the potatoes, put them in a pot with salted cold water. Bring to a boil and let them simmer for 20 to 30 minutes, or until you can slide the tip of a knife all the way through without resistance.

3. Put the flour on the work surface. Then put the warm boiled potatoes in a potato ricer and squeeze them onto the flour (there is no need to peel them as the skin will remain inside the ricer). Wait a few minutes for the potato mash to cool.

4. Add the sea salt and egg, and knead until you get a smooth dough. The dough is ready when it doesn't stick to the surface anymore, but it is still soft and pliable. You may have to add a little more flour to achieve the right consistency, depending on the potatoes you use.

HOMEMADE PASTA MADE SIMPLE

While Potato Gnocchi are made throughout Italy, the preferred sauces vary by region. In the north, you are more likely to eat them with Butter and Sage Sauce (page 174), Gorgonzola Sauce (page 189), and Pesto alla Genovese (page 183); in central Italy, with Ragù alla Bolognese (page 216); and in the south, with a simple Tomato and Basil Sauce (page 182).

5. To save time, you can do this with a stand mixer. Put all of the ingredients together in the bowl of the mixer fitted with a paddle attachment and knead until combined. If the dough is sticky, add a little more flour and knead by hand until it becomes smooth and pliable. The dough is ready when it doesn't stick to your hands.

6. Divide the dough into 8 to 10 balls. Roll each ball of dough into a ⅔-inch-thick rope using your fingertips.

7. Cut the ropes of dough into 1-inch pieces and place them on the prepared baking sheets. If you want, you can give gnocchi their traditional shape by rolling them on the tines of a fork (or on the gnocchi board) while pressing down with your thumb.

8. Repeat the above steps until you have no dough left.

9. Let the gnocchi rest for 15 minutes before cooking them.

TO COOK THE GNOCCHI

1. Set a large pot of salted water on the stove to boil (see page 40) and cook the gnocchi in the boiling water, just as you would cook pasta.

2. The gnocchi are ready as soon as they start to float. This will take 1 to 2 minutes.

3. Remove the gnocchi with a slotted spoon.

4. Depending on the sauce you choose for serving, you can either sauté the gnocchi in the pot with the sauce for a minute or two, or put the gnocchi in a large serving bowl and toss them with the sauce.

5. Serve immediately.

TIP: Dry, starchy potatoes, like russets, make the fluffiest gnocchi. You can also use purple potatoes to make purple gnocchi. The more flour you add, the denser your gnocchi will be.

spinach and ricotta gnudi

Gnudi are a variation on gnocchi from Tuscany, and are different from gnocchi in texture, since they are much softer. Gnudi are basically dumplings made of the spinach and ricotta stuffing used to fill ravioli. They contain very little flour, which makes them much softer than gnocchi. They are called *gnudi*, which means "naked," because they are like ravioli without their pasta cover. Don't you just love their cheeky name? I sure do, but I like their flavor even more! SERVES 4

PREP TIME: 50 MINUTES, PLUS 2 HOURS RESTING TIME | **COOK TIME:** 1 TO 2 MINUTES

EQUIPMENT

Pot to cook the spinach

Large bowl

Knife, nonserrated

3 (10-by-15-inch) baking sheets

Parchment paper

Wooden spoon, to stir the gnudi

Large pot, to cook the gnudi

Slotted spoon, to drain the gnudi

INGREDIENTS

1 pound spinach

⅓ cup water

1¼ cups ricotta cheese, set in a colander to drain for about 2 hours

1 large egg

Pinch ground nutmeg

1 teaspoon sea salt, plus more for cooking the gnudi

1 cup finely grated Parmigiano-Reggiano or Grana Padano cheese

½ cup all-purpose flour (you may require a little more or a little less depending on how moist the ricotta is), divided

TO MAKE THE GNUDI

1. Trim and wash the spinach. Place the spinach leaves, still wet from washing, into a pot. Add ⅓ cup of water and put the pot over medium heat. Cook for 2 to 3 minutes, until the spinach is wilted. Drain well and squeeze all the water out.

2. Cut the cooked spinach very finely with a knife and place it in a large bowl along with the ricotta, egg, nutmeg, sea salt, and Parmigiano-Reggiano or Grana Padano.

3. Add 2 tablespoons of flour and mix well. Add a bit more flour, 1 tablespoon at a time, as needed, until the dough has absorbed all of the liquid and it can hold its shape when made into a ball.

Spinach and Ricotta Gnudi are usually served with Butter and Sage Sauce (page 174) or a simple Tomato and Basil Sauce (page 182)—lighter sauces that don't overpower the delicate taste of the gnudi.

4. Put the mixture in the fridge and let it rest for a couple of hours.

5. Line the baking sheets with parchment paper.

6. After the mixture has rested for a couple of hours, put the remaining flour on a plate. With your hands, make walnut-sized balls with the mixture and roll them in the flour.

7. Transfer the gnudi to the prepared baking sheets.

TO COOK THE GNUDI

1. Set a large pot of salted water on the stove to boil (see page 40) and cook the gnudi in the boiling water, just as you would cook pasta. Do so a few at a time, so they do not break.

2. The gnudi are ready as soon as they start floating. This will take 1 to 2 minutes.

3. Remove the gnudi with a slotted spoon.

4. Serve immediately, topped with the sauce of your choice.

TIP: Do not add a lot of water to the spinach when you wilt it, so that it does not absorb too much liquid. Remember the golden rule: The drier your ingredients, the less flour you will need and the more pillowy your gnocchi and gnudi will be.

butternut squash and potato gnocchi

Making flavored gnocchi is lots of fun, and this variation is particularly tasty. I like that you get the best of both worlds: They are as soft and pillowy as good potato gnocchi should be, and they also have a nutty squash flavor and a beautiful light orange color. **SERVES 4**

PREP TIME: 1 HOUR AND 15 MINUTES | **COOK TIME:** 1 TO 2 MINUTES

EQUIPMENT

Stand mixer (optional)

Gnocchi board (optional)

Potato ricer

Knife, nonserrated

3 (10-by-15-inch) baking sheets

Wooden spoon, to stir the gnocchi

Large pot, to cook the gnocchi

Slotted spoon, to drain the gnocchi

INGREDIENTS

2½ cups all-purpose flour, plus a little more for dusting (to add little by little; you may require more or less depending on the potatoes and squash)

¾ pound skinned and seeded butternut squash

¾ pound russet potatoes, skin on, halved

1 large egg

Pinch grated nutmeg

1 teaspoon sea salt, plus more for cooking the gnocchi

TO MAKE THE GNOCCHI

1. Dust the baking sheets with all-purpose flour.

2. Cut the butternut squash into slices about 2 inches thick and bake it in a preheated oven at 350°F for 30 minutes or until soft.

3. To cook the potatoes, put them in a pot with salted cold water. Bring to a boil and let them simmer for 20 to 30 minutes, or until you can slide the tip of a knife all the way through without resistance.

4. Put the flour on the work surface. Then put the warm boiled potatoes in a potato ricer and squeeze them onto the flour (there is no need to peel them as the skin will remain inside the ricer). Do the same with the cooked squash. Wait a few minutes for the potato and squash mash to cool down.

5. Add the egg, nutmeg, and sea salt, and knead until you get a smooth dough. The dough is ready when it doesn't stick to the surface anymore, but it is still soft and pliable. You may have to add a little more

These Butternut Squash and Potato Gnocchi go very well with Butter and Sage Sauce (page 174), Gorgonzola Sauce (page 189), or Pumpkin and Sausage Sauce (page 208).

flour to achieve the right consistency, depending on the potatoes and squash you use.

6. If you want to save time, you can do this with a stand mixer. Put all the ingredients together in the bowl of the mixer fitted with a paddle attachment and knead until combined. If the dough is sticky, add a little more flour and knead by hand until it becomes smooth and pliable. The dough is ready when it doesn't stick to your hands.

7. Divide the dough into 8 to 10 balls. Roll each ball of dough into ⅔-inch-thick ropes using your fingertips.

8. Cut the ropes of dough into 1-inch pieces and place them on the prepared baking sheets. If you want, you can give gnocchi their traditional shape by rolling them on the tines of a fork (or on the gnocchi board) while pressing down with your thumb.

9. Repeat the above steps until you have no dough left.

10. Let the gnocchi rest for 15 minutes before cooking them.

TO COOK THE GNOCCHI

1. Set a large pot of salted water on the stove to boil (see page 40). Cook the gnocchi in the boiling water, just as you would cook pasta.

2. The gnocchi are ready as soon as they start floating. This will take 1 to 2 minutes.

3. Remove them with a slotted spoon.

4. Depending on the sauce you choose for serving, you can either sauté them in the pot with the sauce for a minute or two, or put the gnocchi in a big serving bowl and mix them with the sauce.

5. Serve immediately.

TIP: For best results, make sure the potatoes and butternut squash are not too warm when kneading the dough, or they will absorb too much flour and your gnocchi will be too dense.

chestnut gnocchi

These are definitely not your everyday gnocchi. Made with chestnut flour, they are very hearty. They are similar to hand-shaped pasta in texture, and they are not as pillowy as regular gnocchi. They have a slightly sweet and nutty flavor that goes very well with melted butter or cheese-based sauces. They are a traditional dish from the Italian Alps, in the valleys that border Switzerland. **SERVES 4**

PREP TIME: 50 MINUTES | **COOK TIME:** 5 TO 7 MINUTES

EQUIPMENT

Stand mixer (optional)

Gnocchi board (optional)

Knife, nonserrated

Plastic wrap, to keep the dough covered

3 (10-by-15-inch) baking sheets

Wooden spoon, to stir the gnocchi

Large pot, to cook the gnocchi

Slotted spoon, to drain the gnocchi

INGREDIENTS

1¼ cups all-purpose flour, plus more for dusting

2½ cups chestnut flour

1 teaspoon sea salt, plus more for cooking the gnocchi

3 ounces grappa or vodka

1 cup lukewarm water

TO MAKE THE GNOCCHI

1. Dust the baking sheets with all-purpose flour.

2. Mix the chestnut and all-purpose flours together and add the teaspoon of sea salt.

3. Add the grappa or vodka and enough lukewarm water to obtain a tough but pliable dough. Add the water little by little and knead well.

4. If you want to save time, you can do this with a stand mixer. Put all the ingredients together in the bowl of the mixer fitted with a paddle attachment and knead until combined. If the dough is sticky, add a little more flour and knead by hand until it becomes smooth and pliable. The dough is ready when it doesn't stick to your hands.

Chestnut Gnocchi are best eaten with Butter and Sage Sauce (page 174) or a sharp-tasting sauce, like Gorgonzola Sauce (page 189).

5. When the dough is ready, make it into a ball, cover it with plastic wrap, and let it rest for 10 to 15 minutes.

6. Divide the dough into 8 to 10 balls. Roll each ball of dough into ⅔-inch-thick ropes using your fingertips.

7. Cut the ropes of dough into 1-inch pieces and place them on the prepared baking sheets. If you want, you can give gnocchi their traditional shape by rolling them on the tines of a fork (or on the gnocchi board) while pressing down with your thumb.

8. Repeat the above steps until you have no dough left.

9. Let the gnocchi rest for 15 minutes before cooking them.

TO COOK THE GNOCCHI

1. Set a large pot of salted water on the stove to boil (see page 40). Cook the gnocchi in the boiling water, just as you would cook pasta.

2. The gnocchi are ready as soon as they start floating. This will take 5 to 7 minutes.

3. Remove them with a slotted spoon.

4. Depending on the sauce you choose for serving, you can either sauté them in the pot with the sauce for a minute or two, or put the gnocchi in a big serving bowl and mix them with the sauce.

5. Serve immediately.

TIP: Chestnut gnocchi take a little longer than regular gnocchi to cook. To make sure they are ready, simply taste one after they start floating.

broccoli gnocchi

I personally love broccoli, and these gnocchi taste great and look even better. This is a relatively new addition to my repertoire, but I can assure you it will become a staple in your kitchen, too. Broccoli has the perfect consistency to be turned into silky, pillowy, and beautifully green gnocchi. **SERVES 4**

PREP TIME: 1 HOUR AND 15 MINUTES | **COOK TIME:** 1 TO 2 MINUTES

EQUIPMENT

Stand mixer (optional)

Gnocchi board (optional)

Potato ricer

Knife, nonserrated

3 (10-by-15-inch) baking sheets

Wooden spoon, to stir the gnocchi

Large pot, to cook the gnocchi

Slotted spoon, to drain the gnocchi

INGREDIENTS

2½ cups all-purpose flour (to add little by little; you may require more or less depending on the broccoli), plus more for dusting

1 pound broccoli florets

2 garlic cloves

½ cup finely grated Pecorino Romano

1 teaspoon sea salt, plus more for cooking the gnocchi

1 large egg

TO MAKE THE GNOCCHI

1. Dust the baking sheets with all-purpose flour.

2. Clean the broccoli florets and cook them, together with the garlic cloves, in salted boiling water until tender. Drain.

3. Put the flour on the work surface. Then put the warm boiled broccoli and garlic in a potato ricer. When you start ricing, the broccoli will release a lot of liquid, so before squeezing it onto the flour, do an initial squeezing on a separate plate until the excess liquid has been removed. This will ensure your dough will not require too much flour. Wait a few minutes for the broccoli mash to cool down.

4. Add the Pecorino Romano, sea salt, and egg, and knead until you get a smooth dough. You may have to add a little more flour. The dough is ready when it doesn't stick to the surface anymore, but it is still soft and pliable.

You can serve Broccoli Gnocchi with Aglione Sauce (page 194), with a simple Tomato and Basil Sauce (page 182), or with Butter and Sage Sauce (page 174).

5. If you want to save time, you can do this with a stand mixer. Put all the ingredients together in the bowl of the mixer fitted with a paddle attachment and knead until combined. If the dough is sticky, add a little more flour and knead by hand until it becomes smooth and pliable. The dough is ready when it doesn't stick to your hands.

6. Divide the dough into 8 to 10 balls. Roll each ball of dough into ⅔-inch-thick ropes using your fingertips.

7. Cut the ropes of dough into 1-inch pieces and place them on the prepared baking sheets. If you want, you can give gnocchi their traditional shape by rolling them on the tines of a fork (or on the gnocchi board) while pressing down with your thumb.

8. Repeat the above steps until you have no dough left.

9. Let the gnocchi rest for 15 minutes before cooking them.

TO COOK THE GNOCCHI

1. Set a large pot of salted water on the stove to boil (see page 40). Cook the gnocchi in the boiling water, just as you would cook pasta.

2. The gnocchi are ready as soon as they start floating. This will take 1 to 2 minutes.

3. Remove them with a slotted spoon.

4. Depending on the sauce you choose for serving, you can either sauté them in the pot with the sauce for a minute or two, or put the gnocchi in a big serving bowl and mix them with the sauce.

5. Serve immediately.

TIP: If serving with Butter and Sage Sauce (page 174), swap the sage for a couple of garlic cloves and top with toasted pine nuts. Serve with grated Pecorino Romano.

pumpkin gnocchi

Pumpkin gnocchi are very easy to make and taste delicious. They are soft and smooth, and very delicate in flavor. These gnocchi have a lovely orange color and they are particularly good during the fall, when pumpkins are at their best. Serve them with a simple sauce to let the earthy, sweet taste of the pumpkin shine. SERVES 4

PREP TIME: 1 HOUR AND 15 MINUTES | **COOK TIME:** 1 TO 2 MINUTES

EQUIPMENT

Stand mixer (optional)

Gnocchi board (optional)

Cutting board

Potato ricer

Knife, nonserrated

3 (10-to-15-inch) baking sheets

Wooden spoon, to stir the gnocchi

Large pot, to cook the gnocchi

Slotted spoon, to drain the gnocchi

INGREDIENTS

9½ ounces all-purpose flour (to add little by little; you may require more or less depending on the pumpkin), plus more for dusting

2 pounds skinned and seeded pumpkin

1 teaspoon sea salt, plus more for cooking the gnocchi

Pinch grated nutmeg

1 large egg

TO MAKE THE GNOCCHI

1. Dust the baking sheets with all-purpose flour.

2. Cut the pumpkin into slices about 2 inches thick and bake in a preheated oven at 350°F for 30 minutes or until soft.

3. Put the flour on the work surface. Then put the warm pumpkin in a potato ricer and squeeze it onto the flour. Wait a few minutes for the pumpkin mash to cool down.

4. Add the sea salt, nutmeg, and egg, and knead until you get a smooth dough. The dough is ready when it doesn't stick to the surface anymore, but it is still soft and pliable. You may have to add a little more flour to achieve the right consistency, depending on the pumpkin you use.

Pumpkin Gnocchi are perfect with Butter and Sage Sauce (page 174), but they also go very well with Gorgonzola Sauce (page 189).

5. If you want to save time, you can do this with a stand mixer. Put all the ingredients together in the bowl of the mixer fitted with a paddle attachment and knead until combined. If the dough is sticky, add a little more flour and knead by hand until it becomes smooth and pliable. The dough is ready when it doesn't stick to your hands.

6. Divide the dough into 8 to 10 balls. Roll each ball of dough into ⅔-inch-thick ropes using your fingertips.

7. Cut the ropes of dough into 1-inch pieces and place them on the prepared baking sheets. If you want, you can give gnocchi their traditional shape by rolling them on the tines of a fork (or on the gnocchi board) while pressing down with your thumb.

8. Repeat the above steps until you have no dough left.

9. Let the gnocchi rest for 15 minutes before cooking them.

TO COOK THE GNOCCHI

1. Set a large pot of salted water on the stove to boil (see page 40). Cook the gnocchi in the boiling water, just as you would cook pasta.

2. The gnocchi are ready as soon as they start floating. This will take 1 to 2 minutes.

3. Remove them with a slotted spoon.

4. Depending on the sauce you choose for serving, you can either sauté them in the pot with the sauce for a minute or two, or put the gnocchi in a big serving bowl and mix them with the sauce.

5. Serve immediately.

TIP: For best results, use a drier pumpkin variety, such as Italian Tonda Padana. Do not use a food processor to mash the pumpkin or it will become soupy.

beet gnocchi

In this recipe, beets add a modern twist to the classic Ricotta Gnocchi (page 150), and they have a beautiful, intense pink color. The slight sweetness that the beets add to these pillowy gnocchi is perfectly balanced by serving them with a sharp, cheesy sauce. Blue or goat's cheese would be the perfect accompaniment. **SERVES 4**

PREP TIME: 50 MINUTES | **COOK TIME:** 1 TO 2 MINUTES

EQUIPMENT

Stand mixer (optional)

Gnocchi board (optional)

Food processor

Big bowl

Knife, nonserrated

3 (10-by-15-inch) baking sheets

Wooden spoon, to stir the gnocchi

Large pot, to cook the gnocchi

Slotted spoon, to drain the gnocchi

INGREDIENTS

2 cups all-purpose flour (to add little-by-little, you may require more or less depending on how moist the ricotta is), plus more for dusting

1 large or 2 medium beets

1 cup ricotta, drained

1 large egg

1 teaspoon sea salt, plus more for cooking the gnocchi

⅔ cup finely grated Parmigiano-Reggiano or Grana Padano

TO MAKE THE GNOCCHI

1. Dust the baking sheets with all-purpose flour and preheat the oven to 400°F.

2. Wrap the beet in foil and bake for about 1 hour, or until tender and cooked through. When ready, peel and let it cool down completely. Purée the cooked beet in a food processor.

3. Put the ricotta, egg, sea salt, pureed beet, and Parmigiano-Reggiano or Grana Padano in a big bowl.

4. Slowly add the flour and start kneading. You may have to add a little more flour to achieve the right consistency. The dough is ready when it doesn't stick to your hands, but it is still soft and pliable.

5. If you want to save time, you can do this with a stand mixer. Put all the ingredients together in the bowl of the mixer fitted with a paddle attachment and knead until combined. If the dough is sticky, add a little more flour and knead by hand until it becomes smooth and pliable. The dough is ready when it doesn't stick to your hands.

Beet Gnocchi are best eaten with a sharp sauce, like Gorgonzola Sauce (page 189), or a simple Butter and Sage Sauce (page 174).

6. Divide the dough into 8 to 10 balls. Roll each ball of dough into ⅔-inch-thick ropes using your fingertips.

7. Cut the ropes of dough into 1-inch pieces and place them on the prepared baking sheets. If you want, you can give gnocchi their traditional shape by rolling them on the tines of a fork (or on the gnocchi board) while pressing down with your thumb.

8. Repeat the above steps until you have no dough left.

9. Let the gnocchi rest for 15 minutes before cooking them.

TO COOK THE GNOCCHI

1. Set a large pot of salted water on the stove to boil (see page 40). Cook the gnocchi in the boiling water, just as you would cook pasta.

2. The gnocchi are ready as soon as they start floating. This will take 1 to 2 minutes.

3. Remove them with a slotted spoon.

4. Depending on the sauce you choose for serving, you can either sauté them in the pot with the sauce for a minute or two, or put the gnocchi in a big serving bowl and mix them with the sauce.

5. Serve immediately.

TIP: If you don't want to cook your own beets, the store-bought, precooked variety works perfectly for this recipe.

gnocchi alla romana

Gnocchi alla Romana is a traditional dish from Rome, as the name suggests. They are apparently the first kind of gnocchi ever made, as they date back (in a very similar form) to the Roman Empire. These gnocchi are made with semolina flour and milk, cut into rounds, and then baked with Parmigiano-Reggiano and butter until golden brown. They are some of the best comfort food Italy has to offer. They are really easy to make and they freeze beautifully, so I always make extra. SERVES 4

PREP TIME: 30 MINUTES | **COOK TIME:** 20 MINUTES

EQUIPMENT

Parchment paper

2½-inch round pasta cutter

2 10-by-15-inch baking sheets

Wooden spoon, to stir the semolina flour

Large pot, to cook the semolina flour

13-by-9-inch baking dish, to bake the gnocchi

INGREDIENTS

7 tablespoons unsalted butter, divided, plus additional for preparing the baking dish

4 cups milk

¼ teaspoon grated nutmeg

Sea salt

1½ cups semolina flour

3 large egg yolks

1⅓ cup finely grated Parmigiano-Reggiano, divided

TO MAKE THE GNOCCHI

1. Cover the baking sheets with parchment paper and lightly butter the baking dish.

2. Put the milk, four tablespoons of butter, and nutmeg in a large pot, season with sea salt, and bring to a boil. Add the semolina flour and keep stirring. Cook over medium heat, stirring constantly, for about 10 minutes, or until the mixture thickens.

3. Remove the pot from the heat and add the egg yolks, one at a time, stirring until well combined. Add ⅔ cup of Parmigiano-Reggiano and stir well.

4. Pour the mixture onto the prepared baking sheets and spread it into ½-inch-thick sheets. Let it cool down until it firms up, 20 to 30 minutes.

5. Using a round pasta cutter, cut out rounds of 2½ inches in diameter. Put them in a greased baking dish, making sure to slightly overlap them.

Gnocchi alla Romana are traditionally served baked, like in the above recipe. If you prefer, you can add some dried herbs, like sage or thyme, to give the final dish extra flavor.

TO COOK THE GNOCCHI

1. Preheat a fan-forced oven to 395°F or a conventional oven to 430°F.

2. Sprinkle the gnocchi with the remaining ⅔ cup of Parmigiano-Reggiano and top with the remaining 3 tablespoons of butter. At this point, if you want, you can freeze the semolina gnocchi. (See Tip.)

3. Bake in the preheated oven for 20 minutes, or until golden brown. Serve immediately.

TIP: This dish freezes really well. Assemble it per the directions above, cover the baking dish with foil, and freeze. To cook, bake from frozen, adding a few extra minutes in the oven so that it browns.

canederli

Canederli, also known locally as *knödel*, are bread gnocchi typical of the area of South Tyrol, at the border with Austria. Resembling a matzo ball in shape and texture, similar versions are found in Austrian, German, Hungarian, Croatian, and Czech cuisines. The classic Italian recipe calls for Italian speck, which is a smoked prosciutto made in South Tyrol. Canederli are traditionally served in broth, or with melted butter and sage as a main course, instead of pasta. They are the perfect comfort food, especially on a cold evening. SERVES 4

PREP TIME: 30 MINUTES, 1 HOUR RESTING TIME | **COOK TIME:** 15 MINUTES

EQUIPMENT

Big bowl

Knife, nonserrated

Cutting board

2 10-by-15-inch baking sheets

Parchment paper

Skillet

Wooden spoon, to stir the canederli

Large pot, to cook the canederli

Slotted spoon, to drain the canederli

INGREDIENTS

1 tablespoon unsalted butter

1 tablespoon finely chopped onion

5 ounces Italian speck, cut into ⅛-inch cubes

9 ounces stale white crusty bread, cut into ¼-inch cubes

2 large eggs, lightly whisked

1 cup milk

2 tablespoons chopped flat-leaf parsley

Sea salt, plus more for cooking the canederli

Freshly ground black pepper

¼ cup all-purpose flour (and some breadcrumbs if required)

Canederli are served either in Italian Chicken Broth (page 201) or with Butter and Sage Sauce (page 174). In either case, pour the sauce on top of the canederli directly in the serving bowls.

TO MAKE THE CANEDERLI

1. Melt the butter in the skillet over medium-low heat. Add the onion and sauté for 2 minutes, or until translucent. Add the speck and sauté for 2 to 3 more minutes. Remove from the heat and let cool.

2. Put the cubed bread in a large bowl. Add the speck-and-onion mixture to it along with the eggs. Add the milk and parsley, and season with sea salt and freshly ground black pepper. Mix well, but gently, with your hands.

3. Let the mixture rest for 1 hour, mixing occasionally.

4. Add the flour and mix well. The mixture should be soft, but firm enough to make it into balls. If it does not hold its shape, add some breadcrumbs to the mixture.

5. To shape canederli, gently make 8 balls with the bread mixture. Set the balls aside on baking sheets covered with parchment paper until you are ready to cook them.

TO COOK THE CANEDERLI

1. Set a large pot of salted water on the stove to boil (see page 40). Add the canederli to the boiling water and reduce the heat to low (the water should simmer but not boil). Simmer for 15 minutes.

2. When ready, remove them with a slotted spoon.

3. Serve 2 canederli per person topped with the sauce of your choice.

TIP: Italian speck is traditionally the preferred choice for this recipe, but if you cannot find it where you live, you can substitute it with pancetta, Prosciutto di Parma, or any other smoked cold cut.

gorgonzola-stuffed potato gnocchi

Stuffed potato gnocchi are the king of gnocchi. There is nothing better than to bite into soft, pillowy potato gnocchi to find a gooey surprise. These gnocchi are a bit bigger than the traditional ones, which works better for those who love cheese: The bigger, the more stuffing you can put inside! Easy, yet sophisticated, they are perfect for any special occasion. Serve them with some Parmigiano-Reggiano on the top for the perfect experience! **SERVES 4**

PREP TIME: 1 HOUR AND 15 MINUTES | **COOK TIME:** 2 TO 3 MINUTES

EQUIPMENT

3 (10-by-15-inch) baking sheets

Potato ricer

Stand mixer (optional)

Knife, nonserrated

Gnocchi board (optional)

Wooden spoon, to stir the gnocchi

Large pot, to cook the gnocchi

Slotted spoon, to drain the gnocchi

INGREDIENTS

1 cup all-purpose flour (to add little by little; you may require more or less depending on the potatoes), plus more for dusting

2¼ pounds russet potatoes, skin on, halved

¾ teaspoon sea salt, plus more for cooking the gnocchi

1 large egg

3½ ounces Gorgonzola cheese

TO MAKE THE GNOCCHI

1. Dust the baking sheets with all-purpose flour.

2. To cook the potatoes, put them in a pot with salted cold water. Bring to a boil and let them simmer for 20 to 30 minutes, or until you can slide the tip of a knife all the way through without resistance.

3. Put the flour on the work surface. Then put the warm boiled potatoes in a potato ricer and squeeze them onto the flour (there is no need to peel them as the skin will remain inside the ricer). Wait a few minutes for the potato mash to cool down.

4. Add the sea salt and the egg, and knead until you get a smooth dough. The dough is ready when it doesn't stick to the surface anymore, but it is still soft and pliable. You may have to add a little more flour to achieve the right consistency, depending on the potatoes you use.

Gorgonzola-Stuffed Potato Gnocchi are best served with lighter sauces, like Butter and Sage Sauce (page 174), so the flavor of the stuffing shines.

5. If you want to save time, you can do this with a stand mixer. Put all the ingredients together in the bowl of the mixer fitted with a paddle attachment and knead until combined. If the dough is sticky, add a little more flour and knead by hand until it becomes smooth and pliable. The dough is ready when it doesn't stick to your hands.

6. Divide the dough into 8 to 10 balls. Roll each ball of dough into 1-inch-thick ropes using your fingertips.

7. Cut the ropes of dough into 1-inch pieces.

8. Flatten them slightly with your fingers. Put about ¼ teaspoon of Gorgonzola in the center and then roll it back into an oval-shaped ball and place on the prepared baking sheets. If you want, you can give gnocchi their traditional shape by rolling them on the ribs of a fork (or on the gnocchi board) while pressing down with your thumb. Be gentle or the stuffing may leak out.

9. Repeat the above steps until you have no dough left.

10. Let the gnocchi rest for 15 minutes before cooking them.

TO COOK THE GNOCCHI

1. Set a large pot of salted water on the stove to boil (see page 40). Cook the gnocchi in the boiling water, just as you would cook pasta.

2. The gnocchi are ready as soon as they start floating. This will take 2 or 3 minutes.

3. Remove them with a slotted spoon.

4. Depending on the sauce you choose for serving, you can either sauté them in the pot with the sauce for a minute or two, or put the gnocchi in a big serving bowl and mix them with the sauce.

5. Serve immediately.

TIP: If you are not a fan of blue cheese, you can substitute any other creamy cheese. Taleggio or stracchino would also be perfect choices for this recipe.

chapter 8

SAUCES

N OW THAT YOU KNOW how to make all kinds of homemade pasta, from simple hand-shaped cavatelli to the more difficult stuffed varieties, you are ready to cook your pasta and enjoy it. You will finally be able to taste your creations and serve them with the most suitable sauces.

In this last chapter, you will find the recipes for mouthwatering pasta sauces, so that you are not left wondering how to serve your pasta after all the hard work you have put into it. You will find modern recipes for sauce, as well as classics, like Cacio e Pepe (page 180), Pesto alla Genovese (page 183), Ragù alla Bolognese (page 216), and Arrabbiata (page 195), all listed in order from the easiest to the most difficult. Since some sauces go better with specific pasta shapes, I have added suggestions about what pasta to serve with each sauce; however, feel free to mix and match to suit your taste buds.

<< LEFT: RAGÙ ALLA BOLOGNESE (PAGE 216)

butter and sage sauce

This recipe is a staple of Italian cuisine. It is a very basic sauce that can be used to serve a huge variety of pasta shapes. It works well with soft pasta, like gnudi and gnocchi, and is perfect for stuffed pasta with a delicate filling, because the sauce will not overpower the taste of the filling. **SERVES 4**

PREP TIME: 2 MINUTES | **COOK TIME:** 3 MINUTES

EQUIPMENT

Saucepan

Large pot, to cook the pasta

Wooden spoon, to stir the pasta

Colander, to drain the pasta

INGREDIENTS

¼ cup plus 3 tablespoons unsalted butter

8 sage leaves

Sea salt

4 tablespoons finely grated Parmigiano-Reggiano, plus more to serve

Freshly ground black pepper, to serve

1. Heat the butter, sage, and sea salt in a saucepan over low heat until the butter melts. Remove the pan from the heat.

2. When the pasta is cooked, drain it and put it back in the pot over low heat.

3. Add the butter and sage sauce and the grated Parmigiano-Reggiano to the pasta. Mix well while cooking for 1 minute.

4. Serve immediately with finely grated Parmigiano-Reggiano and freshly ground black pepper on the top.

GREAT WITH: Stuffed Pasta (page 109) or Gnocchi and Gnudi (page 149).

TIP: You can also add some crushed garlic to the basic sauce to give it a little extra flavor. If you want, you can also brown the butter slightly, to make a sauce with a nuttier taste.

tuna, ricotta, and olive sauce

In my opinion, this is the perfect sauce for egg pasta. This recipe is very dear to my heart because it reminds me of when I used to make pasta with my parents—this would often be our sauce of choice! After spending time making pasta, having a quick sauce to go with it makes perfect sense. All the flavors and textures balance each other beautifully. Serve it with a generous amount of grated Parmigiano-Reggiano on the top. **SERVES 4**

PREP TIME: 5 MINUTES

EQUIPMENT

Big serving bowl

Fork

Large pot, to cook the pasta

Wooden spoon, to stir the pasta

Colander, to drain the pasta

INGREDIENTS

10 ounces ricotta

6 ounces canned tuna, drained and crumbled

20 black olives, pitted and halved

Grated zest of ½ lemon

Sea salt

Freshly ground black pepper

Finely grated Parmigiano-Reggiano, to serve

1. While your pasta is cooking, put the ricotta in a big serving bowl and mash it well with a fork. Add the tuna, olives, and grated lemon zest. Add enough pasta cooking water to obtain a runny cream. Season with sea salt and freshly ground black pepper, and stir to mix.

2. When the pasta is done, drain it, reserving some of the pasta cooking water.

3. Add the cooked pasta to the ricotta mixture and stir to mix. You may need to add a bit of the reserved pasta cooking water if required.

4. Serve immediately with finely grated Parmigiano-Reggiano on the top.

GREAT WITH: Tagliatelle (page 92), Fettuccine (page 90), Pappardelle (page 88), and Maltagliati (page 80).

TIP: Tuna canned in olive oil works best with this recipe, as it is more flavorful than the brined version. You can swap black olives with green, if you prefer.

crudaiola sauce

This easy recipe is a modern take on a classic tomato sauce. All the ingredients are raw, simply cut, and mixed together, almost as if you were making a salad out of them and not a pasta sauce. The name *crudaiola* comes from the Italian word *crudo*, which means "raw." You can use your favorite herbs by substituting them for the basil. Mint, parsley, or even oregano work well here. It's up to you and what you have available in your kitchen. This sauce is best made in summer when tomatoes are ripe and flavorful. **SERVES 4**

PREP TIME: 5 MINUTES

EQUIPMENT

Big serving bowl

Large pot, to cook the pasta

Wooden spoon, to stir the pasta

Colander, to drain the pasta

INGREDIENTS

1½ pounds cherry tomatoes, quartered

2 garlic cloves, halved

12 fresh basil leaves

⅓ cup extra-virgin olive oil

Sea salt

Freshly ground black pepper

Finely grated ricotta salata or Pecorino Romano, to serve (optional)

1. While your pasta is cooking, put the tomatoes, garlic, basil, and oil in a big serving bowl and toss to mix. Season with sea salt and freshly ground black pepper.

2. When the pasta is cooked, drain it and mix it with the sauce.

3. Serve immediately with finely grated ricotta salata or Pecorino Romano on the top (optional).

GREAT WITH: Orecchiette (page 72), Strascinati (page 60), Cavatelli (page 46), and Cicatelli (page 50).

TIP: Prepare the sauce 20 minutes beforehand, so that all the flavors can develop and mix together.

aglio, olio, e peperoncino sauce

Pasta with *aglio, olio, e peperoncino*—garlic, oil, and red pepper flakes—is one of those dishes that every Italian knows how to make from a very young age. It is our go-to recipe for a last-minute meal, better if it's going to be shared with friends. It's made with pantry staples, so it can be made on the spot, without having to run to the store for that special missing ingredient. This is definitely a recipe you should memorize. SERVES 4

PREP TIME: 5 MINUTES | **COOK TIME:** 5 MINUTES

EQUIPMENT

Skillet

Large pot, to cook the pasta

Wooden spoon, to stir the pasta

Colander, to drain the pasta

INGREDIENTS

¼ cup extra-virgin olive oil, plus more to drizzle

4 to 6 garlic cloves, chopped

1 teaspoon red pepper flakes

2 tablespoons chopped flat-leaf parsley (optional)

Sea salt

Toasted breadcrumbs or finely grated Pecorino Romano, to serve

1. Heat the oil in a skillet over medium-low heat. Add the garlic and red pepper flakes and sauté for about 1 minute, or until fragrant. Make sure not to burn the garlic or the sauce will taste bitter. Add the parsley and season with sea salt. Stir and remove the pan from the heat.

2. When the pasta is cooked, drain it and add it to the skillet with the sauce. Mix well and drizzle with some additional extra-virgin olive oil if required.

3. Serve immediately, topped with toasted breadcrumbs or finely grated Pecorino Romano.

GREAT WITH: Spaghetti alla Chitarra (page 106), Tagliolini (page 102), Trenette (page 100), and Stringozzi (page 104).

TIP: You can also make a raw version of the above sauce. Simply crush the garlic and put it in a big serving bowl together with the red pepper flakes and extra-virgin olive oil. Mix and let the oil infuse for 20 minutes before tossing it with your pasta.

bucaiola sauce

This is a very quick sauce to make for your homemade pasta. It is a mixture of softened butter, garlic, and herbs that melts when mixed with warm cooked pasta, infusing it with all its aroma. You can prepare this sauce while waiting for the water of the pasta to boil—that's how quick it is to make! **SERVES 4**

PREP TIME: 5 MINUTES

EQUIPMENT

Fork

Mortar and pestle or a chef's knife

Big serving bowl

Large pot, to cook the pasta

Wooden spoon, to stir the pasta

Colander, to drain the pasta

INGREDIENTS

2 or 3 garlic cloves

2 tablespoons chopped flat-leaf parsley

½ cup unsalted butter, at room temperature

Sea salt

Finely grated Pecorino Romano, to serve (optional)

1. Using a mortar and pestle, or the back of a chef's knife, mash together the garlic and parsley until you get a rough paste.

2. In a big serving bowl, work the butter with a fork until creamy. Add the garlic and parsley paste and mix well. Season with sea salt.

3. When the pasta is cooked, drain it and mix it with the sauce. Toss until the sauce has thoroughly melted and the pasta is evenly coated.

4. Serve immediately with finely grated Pecorino Romano on the top, if you like.

GREAT WITH: Pici (page 54), Stringozzi (page 104), and Spaghetti alla Chitarra (page 106).

TIP: You can also use salted butter for this recipe, but if you do, be careful not to add too much salt to the mixture.

walnut sauce

Together with Pesto alla Genovese (page 183), this is another typical recipe from Genoa, a city in the North of Italy. It is a no-cook sauce, so it is perfect to make on a busy evening or a hot summer day. In Italy, you can buy it from shops that sell freshly made pasta, as it goes really well with a few fresh pasta shapes, but it can be easily made at home. **SERVES 4**

PREP TIME: 10 MINUTES

EQUIPMENT

Food processor

Bowl

Spoon

Large pot, to cook the pasta

Wooden spoon, to stir the pasta

Colander, to drain the pasta

INGREDIENTS

½ garlic clove

5 tablespoons walnuts

1½ teaspoons chopped flat-leaf parsley

1 slice white sandwich bread, soaked in milk

6 tablespoons milk, plus additional if needed

Sea salt

2 tablespoons extra-virgin olive oil

Finely grated Parmigiano-Reggiano (optional)

1. Put the garlic, walnuts, parsley, soaked bread, and milk in a food processor and process until the sauce is finely ground. Season with sea salt.

2. Transfer to a bowl, add the oil, and stir to mix. You may need to add a little extra milk, depending on how much liquid the bread has absorbed. The sauce should be creamy, similar to pesto in consistency.

3. When the pasta is cooked, drain it and mix it with the sauce. Add a little more extra-virgin olive oil if required.

4. Serve immediately with finely grated Parmigiano-Reggiano on the top (optional).

GREAT WITH: Trofie (page 62), Trenette (page 100), and Ricotta Gnocchi (page 150).

TIP: This sauce can be made using different herbs. Try swapping the chopped parsley for fresh thyme, for example. You can also substitute the walnuts with either almonds or hazelnuts for a different taste.

cacio e pepe sauce

Cacio e pepe is one of the most famous pasta dishes from Rome. There is no local *trattoria* that doesn't have this pasta on the menu, and people adore it. The good news is you don't have to go all the way to Rome to enjoy an authentic plate of pasta with cacio e pepe (which, by the way, simply means "cheese and pepper")! Follow my recipe and you will be able to make this creamy, delicious, and simple dish at home. **SERVES 4**

PREP TIME: 5 MINUTES

EQUIPMENT

Big serving bowl

Fork

Ladle

Large pot, to cook the pasta

Wooden spoon, to stir the pasta

Colander, to drain the pasta

INGREDIENTS

2 cups finely grated Pecorino Romano

3 to 4 teaspoons freshly ground black pepper

Sea salt

1. Put the grated Pecorino Romano and freshly ground black pepper in a big serving bowl and mix with a fork.

2. Cook your pasta as per the instructions on page 40. One minute before the pasta is cooked, scoop out 2 ladles of the pasta cooking water and pour it over the cheese and pepper mixture. Mix well with a fork and season with sea salt.

3. Drain the pasta (reserving a little more of the pasta cooking water) and mix it in the bowl with the sauce. Add a little more pasta cooking water if required.

4. Serve immediately.

GREAT WITH: Spaghetti alla Chitarra (page 106), Tagliolini (page 102), Trenette (page 100), Stringozzi (page 104), and Spinach and Ricotta Ravioli Tondi (page 113).

TIP: Keep the pasta and the sauce a little runnier than you normally would. Serve as soon as possible, or the sauce will dry out and the pasta will stick together.

sun-dried tomato sauce

This bold-flavored pasta sauce comes together in under 10 minutes. I learned how to make it in Sicily, where you can find some of the best sun-dried tomatoes and capers in the whole world. In fact, the small Sicilian island of Pantelleria, which is closer to Africa than to Italy, is famous throughout the world for its wild capers. This sauce is especially great for short pasta. **SERVES 4**

PREP TIME: 5 MINUTES | **COOK TIME:** 5 MINUTES

EQUIPMENT

Skillet

Large pot, to cook the pasta

Wooden spoon, to stir the pasta

Colander, to drain the pasta

INGREDIENTS

¼ cup extra-virgin olive oil, plus more to drizzle

2 garlic cloves, halved

½ pound sun-dried tomatoes, chopped

⅓ cup capers, drained and rinsed

1 teaspoon dried oregano

Sea salt

Freshly ground black pepper

Finely grated Pecorino Romano, to serve

1. Heat the oil in a skillet over medium-low heat. Add the garlic and sauté for about 1 minute, or until fragrant. Make sure not to burn the garlic or the sauce will taste bitter. Add the sun-dried tomatoes, capers, and oregano. Season with sea salt and freshly ground black pepper. Stir and cook for 2 to 3 minutes. Remove from the heat.

2. When the pasta is cooked, drain it and add it to the skillet with the sauce. Mix well and drizzle with a bit more extra-virgin olive oil if desired.

3. Serve immediately with finely grated Pecorino Romano on the top.

GREAT WITH: Orecchiette (page 72), Strascinati (page 60), Cavatelli (page 46), Garganelli (page 74), and Farfalle (page 52).

TIP: Taste the sauce before adding any salt—sun-dried tomatoes and capers can already be quite salty, so you may not need any extra.

tomato and basil sauce

This sauce is at the base of Italian cooking. It is possibly the most universal sauce of all, and it can be used with any pasta shape, gnocchi and gnudi included. It is very easy to make, and you can use it as the base for many other sauces. You can swap the onion for garlic if you like, or add other ingredients to turn it into something new every time you make it. It's usually a kids' favorite as well, so it is a real family pleaser. **SERVES 4**

PREP TIME: 5 MINUTES | **COOK TIME:** 20 MINUTES

EQUIPMENT

Knife

Cutting board

Saucepan

Large pot, to cook the pasta

Wooden spoon, to stir the pasta

Colander, to drain the pasta

INGREDIENTS

¼ cup extra-virgin olive oil

½ onion, chopped

1 (28-ounce) can diced tomatoes

¼ cup water

Sea salt

5 or 6 fresh basil leaves

Finely grated Parmigiano-Reggiano, to serve

1. Heat the olive oil in the saucepan over low heat. Add the onion and sauté for 2 minutes, or until translucent. Add the tomatoes and water. Season with sea salt, cover, and cook for 10 to 15 minutes over low heat. Add the basil leaves and stir. Remove the pan from the heat.

2. When the pasta is cooked, drain it and put it back in the pot over low heat.

3. Add the tomato and basil sauce and mix well while cooking on low for 1 minute.

4. Serve immediately with finely grated Parmigiano-Reggiano on the top.

GREAT WITH: All kinds of pasta in this book.

TIP: In summer, when tomatoes are in season, you can make this sauce with fresh, ripe tomatoes. Simply make a cross with a knife at the bottom of each tomato, put it in boiling water for 2 minutes, and peel and seed it. Chop and use as per the above recipe.

pesto alla genovese

Pesto alla Genovese is the most well-known type of pesto both in Italy and abroad. It is a typical recipe from Genoa, in Northern Italy, and I remember stuffing myself with it every time I was in the area! It is such a common sauce that nowadays you can also find it ready-made in many stores. However, this homemade version tastes a lot better, and it requires only 10 minutes to make! Almost every Italian household has its own pesto recipe . . . and this is mine. **SERVES 4**

PREP TIME: 10 MINUTES

EQUIPMENT

Mortar and pestle or food processor

Big serving bowl

Spoon

Large pot, to cook the pasta

Wooden spoon, to stir the pasta

Colander, to drain the pasta

INGREDIENTS

1 medium garlic clove

1 tablespoon pine nuts

Sea salt

2½ cups basil leaves

2 tablespoons very finely grated Parmigiano-Reggiano, plus more for serving

2 tablespoons very finely grated Pecorino Romano, plus more for serving

4 tablespoons extra-virgin olive oil, divided

1. Put the garlic, pine nuts, and a pinch sea salt in the mortar and crush them into a fine paste using the pestle. Add the basil leaves a few at a time and keep crushing the paste until finely ground.

2. To make pesto in a food processor, simply put the garlic, pine nuts, and a pinch sea salt plus 2 tablespoons of olive oil in the processor and blend until just slightly grainy.

3. Transfer the mixture to a large serving bowl. Add the remaining 2 tablespoons of olive oil and both the Parmigiano-Reggiano and Pecorino Romano. Mix well with a spoon and season with sea salt. Cover the sauce with a little extra-virgin olive oil to prevent it from oxidizing and becoming darker in color.

continued >

4. When the pasta is cooked, drain it and mix it with the sauce. Add a little more extra-virgin olive oil if required.

5. Serve immediately with finely grated Parmigiano-Reggiano or Pecorino Romano (or a mix of both) on the top.

GREAT WITH: Trofie (page 62), Trenette (page 100), and Potato Gnocchi (page 152).

TIP: This sauce is very often served with chunks of warm boiled potatoes and green beans. For 4 people, use 2 potatoes and a handful of green beans. Add them to the sauce when mixing it with the pasta.

pesto alla trapanese

Pesto alla Trapanese is the most traditional pasta sauce you can eat in the area of Trapani, in Western Sicily. The sauce is very easy to make, and it is the Trapanese version of the most renowned pesto from Genoa. It is similar to its "green cousin," but it also contains tomatoes, almonds, and much more garlic. In fact, among the locals, this sauce is also known as *pasta cull'agghia*, which in the Sicilian language means "pasta with garlic." I learned how to make this pesto from my grandmother, Nonna Bice. Hers was the best! SERVES 4

PREP TIME: 10 MINUTES

EQUIPMENT

Mortar and pestle or food processor

Big serving bowl

Spoon

Large pot, to cook the pasta

Wooden spoon, to stir the pasta

Colander, to drain the pasta

INGREDIENTS

2 large garlic cloves

5 almonds

Sea salt

1 cup fresh basil leaves

15 ripe cherry tomatoes, halved

¼ cup extra-virgin olive oil

2 tablespoons very finely grated Parmigiano-Reggiano

2 tablespoons very finely grated Pecorino Romano, plus more for serving

1. Put the garlic, almonds, and a pinch sea salt in the mortar and crush them into a fine paste using the pestle. Add the basil leaves a few at a time and keep crushing the paste until finely ground. Add the halved cherry tomatoes a few at a time and mash them well.

2. To make pesto in a food processor, combine the garlic, almonds, and tomatoes and pulse for a few seconds. You want the sauce to remain chunky, so do not blend for too long.

3. Transfer to a serving bowl. Add the oil, Parmigiano-Reggiano, and Pecorino Romano. Mix well with a spoon and season with sea salt.

continued >

4. When the pasta is cooked, drain it and mix it with the sauce.

5. Serve immediately with finely grated Pecorino Romano on the top.

GREAT WITH: Busiati (page 70), Trofie (page 62), and Fusilli Avellinesi (page 68).

TIP: This sauce is very often served topped with fried slices of eggplant. Cut 1 eggplant into ½-inch-thick slices and fry them in hot vegetable oil. Keep them in a colander to drain the excess oil before adding them to the pasta.

prawn and zucchini sauce

This sauce is very delicate and sophisticated. I remember my mother making it often during our holidays in Sicily, as we were able to get amazingly fresh prawns over there. It is a very easy recipe, and the sauce takes just a few minutes to make. The secret to its awesomeness is to use fresh prawns and good-quality extra-virgin olive oil, as these are the ingredients that give the dish its delicious flavor. **SERVES 4**

PREP TIME: 10 MINUTES | **COOK TIME:** 10 MINUTES

EQUIPMENT

Saucepan

Large pot, to cook the pasta

Wooden spoon, to stir the pasta

Colander, to drain the pasta

INGREDIENTS

¼ cup extra-virgin olive oil

½ onion, finely chopped

2 zucchini, chopped into 1-inch pieces

2 tablespoons water

1 pound prawns, peeled, deveined, and roughly chopped

¼ cup white wine

Sea salt

1. Heat the oil in a saucepan over medium-low heat. Add the onion and sauté for a couple of minutes, or until translucent. Be careful not to burn it. Add the zucchini and water. Cover and let cook for 5 minutes, or until the zucchini are tender. Add the prawns and stir.

2. Add the white wine and increase the heat to let the alcohol evaporate. Season with sea salt and cook for a couple of minutes.

3. Remove the pan from the heat and keep it covered until your pasta is cooked.

4. When the pasta is cooked, drain it and mix it with the sauce.

5. Serve immediately.

GREAT WITH: Strozzapreti (page 64), Cozzette (page 58), Tagliolini (page 102), Trenette (page 100), Cicatelli (page 50), and Rombi (page 96).

TIP: You can add some fresh herbs to this basic recipe. Fresh basil and parsley both go very well with it. For a different flavor, add a pinch of saffron instead of the herbs.

lemon sauce

This is a very refreshing pasta sauce typical of Southern Italy, and more specifically, the beautiful Amalfi Coast. The area is very famous for its lemons, which are regularly used in local dishes. After all, it is the exact same area where *limoncello* (a lemon-based liqueur) was born. This sauce comes together in less than 5 minutes, and it is delicate, tangy, creamy, and absolutely delightful. You will be transported to the Amalfi Coast with every bite. **SERVES 4**

PREP TIME: 5 MINUTES | **COOK TIME:** 5 MINUTES

EQUIPMENT

Saucepan

Large pot, to cook the pasta

Wooden spoon, to stir the pasta

Colander, to drain the pasta

INGREDIENTS

2½ tablespoons unsalted butter

Finely grated zest of 2 lemons

Sea salt

Freshly ground black pepper

1 scant cup heavy cream

Finely chopped flat-leaf parsley, for garnish (optional)

Finely grated Parmigiano-Reggiano, to serve

1. Melt the butter in a saucepan over low heat. Add the grated lemon zest, season with sea salt and freshly ground black pepper, and stir well. Remove the pan from the heat.

2. When the pasta is cooked, drain it and put it back in the pot over low heat.

3. Add the lemon sauce and heavy cream and mix well while cooking on low for 1 minute. You may need to add a little warm water (or pasta cooking water) at this point, if the sauce dries up.

4. Serve immediately with finely grated Parmigiano-Reggiano and a sprinkle of chopped parsley on the top.

GREAT WITH: Tagliolini (page 102), Tagliatelle (page 92), Fettuccine (page 90), and Lemon and Ricotta Stelle (page 125).

TIP: As you will be eating the zest, it would be best to use organic lemons for this recipe. Keep your pasta sauce a bit runny because it will thicken by the time you serve the pasta.

gorgonzola sauce

This is a very simple cheese sauce often served with pasta. I especially like to serve gnocchi with it, as I find that the creaminess of the sauce goes very well with the airy texture of gnocchi. For some crunch, you could also add some crushed walnuts or hazelnuts to the pasta served with this sauce. If Gorgonzola is not available, simply swap it for your favorite blue cheese. **SERVES 4**

PREP TIME: 2 MINUTES | **COOK TIME:** 3 MINUTES

EQUIPMENT

Saucepan

Large pot, to cook the pasta

Wooden spoon, to stir the pasta

Colander, to drain the pasta

INGREDIENTS

¾ cup heavy cream

5 ounces Gorgonzola cheese

Sea salt, if required

¼ cup Parmigiano-Reggiano, finely grated plus more to serve

1. Put the cream and Gorgonzola cheese in a saucepan and cook over low heat until the cheese melts, about 2 minutes. Season with sea salt, if required. Remove from the heat.

2. When the pasta is cooked, drain it and put it back in the pot over low heat.

3. Add the Gorgonzola sauce and the grated Parmigiano-Reggiano. Mix well while cooking on low for 1 minute.

4. Serve immediately with some more finely grated Parmigiano-Reggiano on the top.

GREAT WITH: Potato Gnocchi (page 152), Ricotta Gnocchi (page 150), Butternut Squash and Potato Gnocchi (page 156), Pumpkin Gnocchi (page 162), Beet Gnocchi (page 164), and Chestnut Gnocchi (page 158).

TIP: If you don't like Gorgonzola, you can use your favorite soft cheese. If you still want to use Italian cheeses, Taleggio or stracchino work very well. You can also make it with Parmigiano-Reggiano: Simply swap the Gorgonzola for ½ cup grated Parmigiano-Reggiano.

zucchini, chile pepper, and parsley sauce

This quick and nutritious pasta sauce is perfect for a midweek dinner. I like it with long ribbon pasta, especially with Tagliatelle (page 92), as the oil, which is infused with chile peppers and zucchini, mixes with the grated cheese to turn into a delicious cream that clings perfectly to ribbon pasta. **SERVES 4**

PREP TIME: 5 MINUTES | **COOK TIME:** 15 MINUTES

EQUIPMENT

Skillet

Big serving bowl

Large pot, to cook the pasta

Wooden spoon, to stir the pasta

Colander, to drain the pasta

INGREDIENTS

4 medium yellow and green zucchini, cut into ⅛-inch-thick slices

Sea salt

⅔ cup extra-virgin olive oil

½ small red chile pepper, such as cayenne, sliced

1½ teaspoons chopped flat-leaf parsley

Finely grated Parmigiano-Reggiano

1. Season the sliced zucchini with sea salt.

2. Heat the olive oil in a skillet over medium heat. Fry the sliced zucchini in batches, until golden brown on both sides. Make sure not to burn the oil.

3. Transfer the zucchini, along with the remaining cooking oil, to a serving bowl. Add the sliced chile pepper and chopped parsley.

4. When the pasta is cooked, drain it and put it into the serving bowl. Mix and add a little more extra-virgin olive oil, if required.

5. Serve immediately with finely grated Parmigiano-Reggiano on the top.

GREAT WITH: Tagliatelle (page 92), Fettuccine (page 90), Spaghetti alla Chitarra (page 106), and Stringozzi (page 104).

TIP: I use yellow and green zucchini for a touch of extra color, but you can use any kind of zucchini you like.

cream sauce with salmon

You will love this simple yet sophisticated recipe. It's the perfect sauce for any seafood lover and another great midweek dinner idea. I love the combination of garlic and salmon, and the cream helps bring the sauce together. Usually Italians do not put cheese on pasta with fish, but there are a few exceptions, and this is definitely one of them. SERVES 4

PREP TIME: 10 MINUTES | **COOK TIME:** 10 MINUTES

EQUIPMENT

Knife

Cutting board

Saucepan

Large pot, to cook the pasta

Wooden spoon, to stir the pasta

Colander, to drain the pasta

INGREDIENTS

2 tablespoons extra-virgin olive oil

1 garlic clove, chopped

10 ounces boneless salmon fillet, skinned and cut into ½-inch cubes

¼ cup white wine

½ tablespoon finely chopped flat-leaf parsley

Sea salt

¾ cup heavy cream

Finely grated Parmigiano-Reggiano, to serve

Freshly ground black pepper, to serve

1. Heat the oil in a saucepan over medium-low heat. Add the garlic and sauté for 1 minute. Add the salmon and let it cook for 2 minutes. Stir. Add the wine and burn the alcohol off by increasing the heat for a few seconds.

2. Remove the pan from the heat, add the parsley, and season with sea salt.

3. When the pasta is cooked, drain it and put it back in the pot over low heat.

4. Add the salmon sauce and heavy cream, and mix well while cooking on low for 1 minute.

5. Serve immediately with finely grated Parmigiano-Reggiano and freshly ground black pepper on the top.

GREAT WITH: Farfalle (page 52), Garganelli (page 74), Tagliolini (page 102), Maltagliati (page 80), and Rombi (page 96).

TIP: If you prefer, you can swap the fresh salmon for smoked salmon. You can also add 1 tablespoon of tomato purée to the sauce, right before adding the salmon cubes, for a little extra zing and to turn the sauce a pleasant pink color.

creamy mushroom sauce

This is a classic of Italian cuisine. It is very easy to make and will impress even the fussiest eater. You can use the mushrooms of your choice, even though traditionally we use fresh porcini mushrooms. If you cannot find fresh porcini, chanterelles or cremini mushrooms work well, too. This sauce makes for a very hearty and comforting dish, and I love it with a generous amount of grated Parmigiano-Reggiano on the top for extra flavor. SERVES 4

PREP TIME: 10 MINUTES | **COOK TIME:** 10 MINUTES

EQUIPMENT

Skillet

Large pot, to cook the pasta

Wooden spoon, to stir the pasta

Colander, to drain the pasta

INGREDIENTS

2 tablespoons extra-virgin olive oil

1 garlic clove, chopped

9 ounces mushrooms, sliced

¼ cup white wine

1½ teaspoons chopped flat-leaf parsley

Sea salt

¾ cup heavy cream

Finely grated Parmigiano-Reggiano, to serve

Freshly ground black pepper, to serve

1. Heat the olive oil in a skillet over medium-low heat. Add the garlic and sauté for 1 minute. Add the sliced mushrooms, stir, and cook until tender. Add the white wine and burn the alcohol off by increasing the heat for a few seconds.

2. Remove the skillet from the heat. Add the chopped parsley, season with sea salt, and stir. Set the sauce aside.

3. When the pasta is cooked, drain it and put it back into the pot and over low heat.

4. Add the mushroom sauce and heavy cream and mix well. Cook for 1 minute.

5. Serve immediately with finely grated Parmigiano-Reggiano and freshly ground black pepper on the top.

GREAT WITH: Fettuccine (page 90) and Pappardelle (page 88).

TIP: You can also make this sauce using dried porcini. Soak them in a mixture of hot water and milk until soft, strain, and reserve the liquid. Chop the mushrooms and use as per the above recipe. Use the reserved liquid instead of the white wine to flavor the sauce and cook the mushrooms.

cream sauce with ham and peas

This is another traditional Italian recipe. Ham and peas are a very common pairing, and Italians like to use this combination in pasta sauces. It is a favorite of mine as when I was a child, I would often ask my mother to make it for me. This creamy sauce is decadent, elegant, yet a snap to make. It is pure comfort food that will conquer kids and adults alike. **SERVES 4**

PREP TIME: 5 MINUTES | **COOK TIME:** 15 MINUTES

EQUIPMENT

Saucepan

Large pot, to cook the pasta

Wooden spoon, to stir the pasta

Colander, to drain the pasta

INGREDIENTS

2 tablespoons extra-virgin olive oil

2 tablespoons chopped onion

¼ cup chopped honey ham

2 cups fresh or frozen (not thawed) peas

2 to 3 tablespoons water

Sea salt

¾ cup heavy cream

Finely grated Parmigiano-Reggiano, to serve

Freshly ground black pepper, to serve

1. Heat the olive oil in a saucepan over medium-low heat. Add the onion and sauté for 1 minute. Add the ham and peas along with 2 tablespoons of water (if you are using fresh peas, add a bit more water). Stir, cover, and cook on low for 5 minutes or until the peas are soft. Season with sea salt and remove the pan from the heat.

2. When the pasta is cooked, drain it and put it back into the pot over low heat.

3. Add the ham and pea sauce, along with the heavy cream, and mix well. Cook for 1 minute.

4. Serve immediately with finely grated Parmigiano-Reggiano and freshly ground black pepper on the top.

GREAT WITH: Farfalle (page 52), Garganelli (page 74), Pappardelle (page 88), and Ricotta Gnocchi (page 150).

TIP: You can also make this sauce using prosciutto. For a vegetarian version, skip the ham and prosciutto all together. If you want, you can add a pinch of saffron to the sauce to make it more elegant and sophisticated.

aglione sauce

Aglione sauce is traditional fare in Tuscany, particularly in the beautiful town of Siena. It is a very simple red sauce made with tomatoes and lots of garlic. In fact, the name aglione comes from the term *aglio*, which means "garlic." The final result is creamy, garlicky, and only slightly spicy. It is a bold pasta sauce, perfect to eat with many handmade pasta shapes and especially with Pici (page 54). **SERVES 4**

PREP TIME: 5 MINUTES | **COOK TIME:** 20 MINUTES

EQUIPMENT

Saucepan

Large pot, to cook the pasta

Wooden spoon, to stir the pasta

Colander, to drain the pasta

INGREDIENTS

¼ cup extra-virgin olive oil

6 garlic cloves, pressed

½ small red chile pepper, seeded and sliced

¼ cup water

1 (28-ounce) can diced tomatoes

1 tablespoon white wine vinegar

Sea salt

Finely grated Pecorino Romano, to serve

1. Heat the oil in a saucepan over low heat. Add the garlic and chile pepper and sauté for 1 minute. Make sure not to burn the garlic or the sauce will taste bitter. Add the water and let the garlic and chile pepper cook for 2 to 3 minutes longer.

2. Add the tomatoes and vinegar. Season with sea salt, cover, and cook for 10 to 15 minutes on low. Remove the pan from the heat.

3. When the pasta is cooked, drain it and put it back into the pot over low heat.

4. Add the aglione sauce and mix well while cooking for 1 minute.

5. Serve immediately with finely grated Pecorino Romano on the top.

GREAT WITH: Pici (page 54), Broccoli Gnocchi (page 160), and Stringozzi (page 104).

TIP: If your tomatoes are a bit too acidic to begin with, you can add 1 teaspoon of sugar to the sauce to balance out the taste of the vinegar.

arrabbiata sauce

The term *arrabbiata* means "angry" in Italian, and it refers to the spiciness of the chile peppers in this classic Roman pasta sauce. As the ingredients that make up the sauce are few and very simple, it is important to use good-quality products so as to obtain the best results. It is a very popular dish thanks to the fact that it is so easy to prepare. You can find it in all the restaurants of Rome, and now on your table as well! **SERVES 4**

PREP TIME: 5 MINUTES | **COOK TIME:** 20 MINUTES

EQUIPMENT

Saucepan

Large pot, to cook the pasta

Wooden spoon, to stir the pasta

Colander, to drain the pasta

INGREDIENTS

3 tablespoons extra-virgin olive oil

2 garlic cloves, crushed

1 small red chile pepper, sliced

1 (28-ounce) can diced tomatoes

¼ cup water

Sea salt

2 tablespoons chopped flat-leaf parsley

Finely grated Pecorino Romano, to serve

1. Heat the oil in the saucepan over low heat. Add the garlic and chile pepper and sauté for 1 to 2 minutes. Make sure not to burn the garlic or the sauce will taste bitter. Discard the garlic. Add the tomatoes and water. Season with sea salt, cover, and cook on low for 15 minutes. Remove from the heat.

2. When the pasta is cooked, drain it and put it back into the pot over low heat.

3. Add the arrabbiata sauce and chopped parsley, and mix well. Cook for 1 minute.

4. Serve immediately with finely grated Pecorino Romano on the top.

GREAT WITH: Cicatelli (page 50), Maccheroni col Ferretto (page 66), Pici (page 54), and Strozzapreti (page 64).

TIP: Depending on the kind of red chile pepper that you use, you may have to add more or less of it. The sauce should be spicy, but you still want to be able to taste the tomatoes in it.

arugula and tomato sauce

This quick and light sauce, paired with pasta, is perfect for a warm, sunny day. In fact, you can also eat it cold, making it the ideal dish to take on a picnic or to the beach. It is a modern Italian recipe that has become quite trendy in recent years, especially due to the popularity of arugula. Up until a few years ago, arugula was not readily available throughout Italy, but now you can find it everywhere, and using it in pasta sauces has become quite common. SERVES 4

PREP TIME: 5 MINUTES | **COOK TIME:** 15 MINUTES

EQUIPMENT

Saucepan

Large pot, to cook the pasta

Wooden spoon, to stir the pasta

Colander, to drain the pasta

INGREDIENTS

¼ cup plus 2 tablespoons extra-virgin olive oil

2 garlic cloves, halved

¼ teaspoon red pepper flakes

25 cherry tomatoes, halved

2 tablespoons water

6 cups arugula, rinsed

Sea salt

Finely grated ricotta salata or Pecorino Romano, to serve

1. Heat the oil in a saucepan over medium-low heat. Add the garlic and red pepper flakes and sauté for about 1 minute or until fragrant. Make sure not to burn the garlic or the sauce will taste bitter. Add the cherry tomatoes and the water. Stir and cook for 5 minutes. Add the arugula and season with sea salt. Stir and cook for another 5 minutes.

2. When the pasta is cooked, drain it and mix it with the sauce.

3. Serve immediately with finely grated ricotta salata or Pecorino Romano on the top.

GREAT WITH: Orecchiette (page 72), Strascinati (page 60), Cavatelli (page 46), Cicatelli (page 50), and Farfalle (page 52).

TIP: If you prefer, you can use the exact same ingredients without cooking them for a warm pasta salad. Simply chop everything up, mix it together in a serving bowl, and mix your cooked pasta with it.

artichoke sauce

Roman cuisine is very famous for its artichoke recipes. If you visit the eternal city, make sure to order some of the amazing artichoke dishes you will find in the local *trattorie*. In fact, when I last visited Rome, I had the best pasta with artichoke sauce in the Jewish quarter. This recipe recreates that dish to perfection. The recipe itself is pretty straightforward; just make sure to allocate a little extra time to clean the artichokes, especially if you have never done it before. It is not hard, but you need a little patience. **SERVES 4**

PREP TIME: 20 MINUTES | **COOK TIME:** 20 MINUTES

EQUIPMENT

Knife

Cutting board

Big bowl

Saucepan

Large pot, to cook the pasta

Wooden spoon, to stir the pasta

Colander, to drain the pasta

INGREDIENTS

Juice of 2 lemons

4 artichokes

3 tablespoons extra-virgin olive oil

3 garlic cloves, halved

½ cup vegetable stock, divided

1 tablespoon chopped flat-leaf parsley

Sea salt

Freshly ground black pepper

Finely grated Parmigiano-Reggiano, to serve

1. Fill a big bowl with cold water and squeeze the lemon juice into it.

2. Clean the artichokes by removing the tough outer leaves until you get to the lighter yellow leaves. Then cut off the top third of the artichoke and the bottom of the stem. Carefully trim the top and sides of the artichoke. Trim the tough outer portion of the stem by removing the fibrous green exterior. Cut in half and remove the choke (fibrous center). Cut halves into ½-inch slices and place in the lemon water until ready to use. This will prevent the artichokes from oxidizing and turning black. Repeat with remaining artichokes.

3. Heat the oil in a saucepan over medium-low heat. Add the garlic and sauté for about 1 minute, or until fragrant. Make sure not to burn the garlic or the sauce will taste bitter.

continued >

4. Drain the sliced artichokes and add them to the pan. Stir and add most of the vegetable stock (reserve a couple of tablespoons). Season with sea salt and freshly ground black pepper.

5. Cover and cook on medium for 10 to 15 minutes, or until tender. Check halfway through and add the remaining stock if the liquid has evaporated.

6. When the pasta is cooked, drain it and put it back into the pot over low heat.

7. Add the artichoke sauce and parsley and mix well while cooking for 1 minute. You may need to add a little extra stock (or pasta cooking water) at this point, if the sauce dries up.

8. Serve immediately with finely grated Parmigiano-Reggiano on the top.

GREAT WITH: Tagliolini (page 102), Tagliatelle (page 92), and Stringozzi (page 104).

TIP: Besides adding lemon juice to the water, you can also rub the artichokes with lemon while cleaning them. Wear kitchen gloves or rub your hands with lemon juice to prevent your hands from turning black.

broccoli rabe sauce

This is one of the most traditional sauces from the southern Italian region of Apulia and particularly from the town of Bari. It is often associated with orecchiette and strascinati, and I can assure you they are a match made in heaven. It is a very quick recipe to make, and it uses simple ingredients that are easily available to everyone. It is also a great way to get fussy kids to eat some vegetables. SERVES 4

PREP TIME: 15 MINUTES | **COOK TIME:** 30 MINUTES

EQUIPMENT

Large pot, to cook the broccoli rabe and the pasta

Slotted spoon

Saucepan

Wooden spoon, to stir the pasta

Colander, to drain the pasta

INGREDIENTS

2¾ pounds broccoli rabe, trimmed of the tough leaves

5 tablespoons extra-virgin olive oil

3 garlic cloves, crushed

½ small red chile pepper, sliced

4 anchovies, any large bones removed

Sea salt

Finely grated Pecorino Romano or toasted breadcrumbs, to serve

1. Heat a pot of salted water to a slow simmer and add the broccoli rabe. Cook until tender, 10 to 15 minutes. Remove the cooked broccoli rabe with a slotted spoon and reserve the cooking liquid.

2. Heat the oil in a saucepan over medium-low heat. Add the garlic and chile pepper and sauté for 2 minutes. Add the anchovies and break them up with the wooden spoon. Add the cooked broccoli rabe and ¼ cup of the reserved cooking liquid. Mix well. Season with sea salt.

3. Cook the pasta of your choice in the remaining reserved broccoli rabe cooking water. When the pasta is cooked, drain it and put it back into the pot over low heat.

continued >

4. Add the broccoli rabe sauce and mix well. Cook for 1 minute.

5. Serve immediately with finely grated Pecorino Romano or toasted bread-crumbs on the top.

GREAT WITH: Orecchiette (page 72) and Strascinati (page 60).

TIP: If you can't find broccoli rabe where you live, you can swap it for either broc-coli or bok choy. If making with broccoli, use 2 tablespoons toasted pine nuts to top the pasta instead of the breadcrumbs.

italian chicken broth

Chicken broth is another staple of Italian cuisine. We make it to eat with all sorts of small pasta shapes. Every family has its own secret recipe for it, and this is my version. I always make it for Christmas. In fact, in Italy, a typical Christmas Eve dinner always includes stuffed pasta served in chicken broth: It is such a comforting food for a cold winter's night. Use the same quantity of chicken broth to cook your pasta that you would use of water. **SERVES 4**

PREP TIME: 10 MINUTES | **COOK TIME:** 3 HOURS

EQUIPMENT
Large wooden spoon
Large pot
Sieve

INGREDIENTS
4½ pounds chicken bones
1 pound chicken wings
3 onions, peeled
2 carrots
3 large celery stalks
¼ cup chopped flat-leaf parsley
3 bay leaves
5 whole peppercorns
3 cloves
About 1 gallon of water
Sea salt

1. Put the chicken bones and wings in a large pot. Add the onions, carrots, celery, parsley, bay leaves, peppercorns, and cloves. Cover with water.

2. Put the pot on the stove over high heat and bring it to a boil. Reduce the heat to low and simmer, uncovered and without stirring, for 3 hours. Skim off the fat and froth with a spoon every now and then.

3. Strain the broth through a sieve lined with a muslin cloth or a coffee filter.

4. Discard the bones and vegetables.

5. Cook the pasta of your choice in the chicken broth and serve hot.

GREAT WITH: Tortellini Bolognesi (page 140), Spinach and Ricotta Ravioli Tondi (page 113), Cappelletti Romagnoli (page 134), Parmigiano-Reggiano Fagottini (page 129), Quadrucci (page 94), and Canederli (page 168).

TIP: To make a lower-fat chicken broth, simply refrigerate it overnight so that the fat will float up and solidify. Use a slotted spoon to remove the fat layer. Heat up and use. If you have chicken broth left over, transfer it to glass jars and freeze it for later use.

mussel and bean sauce

I know that a sauce that puts together mussels and beans may sound unusual, but it is a very old and traditional recipe from Apulia and Campania. It could be considered an early version of "surf and turf." In reality, our ancestors used to make do with what they had available and created delicious dishes with local produce. Mussels and beans go very well together both in taste and in texture, and complement each other perfectly in this sauce. **SERVES 4**

PREP TIME: 10 MINUTES | **COOK TIME:** 30 MINUTES

EQUIPMENT

2 skillets

Large pot, to cook the pasta

Wooden spoon, to stir the pasta

Colander, to drain the pasta

INGREDIENTS

4 tablespoons extra-virgin olive oil, divided

2 pounds mussels, scrubbed

1 garlic clove, peeled

½ onion, thinly sliced

1 cup canned diced tomatoes

⅓ cup water

1 (16-ounce) can cannellini beans, drained and rinsed

Sea salt

Freshly ground black pepper

2 tablespoons chopped flat-leaf parsley, to serve

1. Put 2 tablespoons of oil, the mussels, and the garlic in a skillet and set it over high heat. Cover and cook until the mussels open, about 2 minutes.

2. Remove most of the mussels from their shells. Keep a few in their shells for decoration. Discard any mussels that do not open.

3. In another skillet, heat the remaining 2 tablespoons of oil over medium-low heat. Add the onion and sauté for about 2 minutes, or until soft. Stir often and make sure it does not burn. Add the tomatoes and the water, and cook for 10 minutes.

4. Add the cannellini beans and mussels, and season with sea salt and freshly ground black pepper. Stir well and cook for 5 more minutes.

5. When the pasta is cooked, drain it and mix it with the sauce.

6. Serve immediately with finely chopped parsley on the top. Decorate with the mussels in the shells.

GREAT WITH: Cozzette (page 58) and Cavatelli (page 46).

TIP: Traditionally, dry beans were used for this recipe, but canned beans help reduce the time required to make this dish without compromising the taste.

chickpea soup

This is one of my all-time favorite soups. Whenever I make it, it takes me back to when I was a child. I grew up in Milan, where winters can be quite cold, and my mother would often make this soup for dinner. It is very easy to make and is hearty and delicious. You can also make it without pasta and eat it with some toasted bread with garlic and extra-virgin olive oil (the simplest bruschetta). I am sure it will bring you the same feeling of warmth that it used to bring me during those cold winter days. SERVES 4

PREP TIME: 10 MINUTES | **COOK TIME:** 30 MINUTES

EQUIPMENT

Food processor

Large pot

Wooden spoon, to stir the pasta

INGREDIENTS

1 pound cooked or canned chickpeas, drained and rinsed, divided

2 tablespoons extra-virgin olive oil, plus more to serve

½ onion, chopped

1 garlic clove, halved

5 cherry tomatoes, halved, or 1 tablespoon diced tomatoes

1 bay leaf

1 sprig rosemary

4 fresh sage leaves

6 cups beef stock

Sea salt

Freshly ground black pepper, to serve

1. Put a third of the chickpeas in a food processor and blend until smooth. Add a bit of stock, if needed, to get a pasty consistency.

2. Heat the oil in a large pot over medium-low heat. Add the onion and garlic and sauté for about 1 minute, or until fragrant. Add the tomatoes, the remaining whole chickpeas, bay leaf, rosemary, and sage, and stir.

3. Stir in the puréed chickpeas and the stock. Season with sea salt. Mix well.

4. Cover and let it cook for 15 minutes.

5. Cook the pasta of your choice in the chickpea soup. Stir often so the pasta doesn't stick to the bottom of the pan. You may need to add some warm water or stock depending on how long your pasta will take to cook. You want to keep the soup a bit runny, as it will thicken once off the heat.

6. Serve warm with freshly ground black pepper on the top and a drizzle of extra-virgin olive oil.

GREAT WITH: Lagane (page 86), Sagne (page 84), and Cavatellini (page 48).

TIP: For a vegetarian version of this dish, swap the beef stock with your favorite vegetable stock. You can also make this soup with your favorite beans.

eggplant and tuna sauce

Eggplant, tuna, and mint: There is nothing more Sicilian than this combination of flavors. Sicily is famous for its amazing fish, including tuna. In fact, both the town of Trapani and the nearby Egadi Islands are renowned all over Italy for their tuna products. This sauce is an ode to my parents' beautiful island, and even though Italians do not usually eat cheese on fish pasta, I like to serve this sauce with some grated Parmigiano-Reggiano on the top. I find that it tastes even better like this. **SERVES 4**

PREP TIME: 40 MINUTES | **COOK TIME:** 30 MINUTES

EQUIPMENT

Knife

Cutting board

Large bowl

Medium pot, to deep-fry eggplant

Saucepan

Slotted spoon

Colander, to drain the eggplant

Large pot, to cook the pasta

Wooden spoon, to stir the pasta

Colander, to drain the pasta

INGREDIENTS

1 medium eggplant, cut into 1-inch cubes

Vegetable oil, for deep-frying (enough for about 3 inches of oil in the pot)

3 tablespoons extra-virgin olive oil

1 onion, thinly sliced

1 (16-ounce) can diced tomatoes

⅓ cup water

6 ounces canned or jarred tuna, drained and crumbled

Sea salt

1 tablespoon finely chopped fresh mint

Finely grated Parmigiano-Reggiano, to serve (optional)

1. Fill a large bowl with salty water and add the cubed eggplant. Let it soak for 30 minutes. This will make it less bitter. Drain the eggplant and dry it well with paper towels.

2. Heat the vegetable oil in a medium pot. When hot, add the eggplant cubes and cook until golden brown, about 3 minutes. Remove with a slotted spoon and drain in a colander placed on top of a plate to remove excess oil.

3. In the meantime, heat the olive oil in a saucepan over medium-low heat. Add the onion and sauté for about 2 minutes or until soft. Stir often and make sure it does not burn. Add the tomatoes and water, and cook for 10 minutes.

4. Add the tuna and season with sea salt. Stir well and cook for 10 more minutes. You may need to add a little water to keep the sauce from drying up.

5. Add the fried eggplant and mint leaves. Stir and remove from the heat.

6. When the pasta is cooked, drain it and mix it with the sauce.

7. Serve immediately with finely grated Parmigiano-Reggiano on the top, if desired.

GREAT WITH: Maltagliati (page 80) and Rombi (page 96).

TIP: You can use your favorite fresh herbs instead of mint. Try fresh basil leaves, parsley, or thyme. You can also swap the eggplant for zucchini, for a sweeter taste.

pumpkin and sausage sauce

When I think of perfect food pairings, one of the first combinations that come to my mind is pumpkin and sausage. I think that both their flavors and textures balance out perfectly. Sausage is bold, a bit spicy and grainy, while pumpkin is delicate, sweet, and smooth. This pasta sauce is the demonstration that pumpkin and sausage together can do wonders! **SERVES 4**

PREP TIME: 10 MINUTES | **COOK TIME:** 20 MINUTES

EQUIPMENT

Immersion blender

Saucepan

Skillet

Large pot, to cook the pasta

Wooden spoon, to stir the pasta

Colander, to drain the pasta

INGREDIENTS

3 tablespoons extra-virgin olive oil, divided

½ onion, chopped

⅔ pound peeled, seeded, and cubed pumpkin

¼ cup water

Sea salt

Freshly ground black pepper

½ pound Italian pork sausage

4 fresh sage leaves

¼ cup white wine

Finely grated Parmigiano-Reggiano, to serve

1. Heat 2 tablespoons of oil in a saucepan over medium-low heat. Add the onion and sauté for about 2 minutes, or until soft. Add the pumpkin and water. Cover and cook until tender. You may have to add some more water depending on the pumpkin you use and how fast it cooks.

2. Purée the pumpkin with an immersion blender until smooth. You may need to add some water to make it into a cream. Season with salt and pepper.

3. Remove the casing from the sausage. Chop the sausage and sauté it in a skillet with the remaining tablespoon of oil and the sage leaves. Brown well, breaking the lumps with a wooden spoon. Add the white wine and raise the heat to burn off the alcohol.

4. When the sausage is cooked, add the puréed pumpkin and mix well.

5. When the pasta is cooked, drain it and put it back into the pot over low heat.

6. Add the pumpkin and sausage sauce and mix well while cooking for 1 minute. You may need to add a little warm water (or pasta cooking water) at this point, if the sauce dries up.

7. Serve immediately with finely grated Parmigiano-Reggiano on the top.

GREAT WITH: Garganelli (page 74), Mafalde (page 98), Fusilli Avellinesi (page 68), and Butternut Squash and Potato Gnocchi (page 156).

TIP: You can swap the sage for a sprig of rosemary or thyme, if you prefer. You can also use butternut squash instead of pumpkin for this recipe.

kale, gorgonzola, and green pesto

This is a strong-flavored pasta sauce that goes really well with short, hand-shaped pasta, especially orecchiette. I love all the different textures and flavors of this sauce: creamy, a little crunchy, sharp, and slightly bitter. This sauce brings all of Italy together on a plate: Gorgonzola from Lombardy, kale from Tuscany, and orecchiette from Apulia. **SERVES 4**

PREP TIME: 15 MINUTES | **COOK TIME:** 30 MINUTES

EQUIPMENT

Knife

Cutting board

Large pot, to cook the kale

Slotted spoon

Saucepan

Food processor

Big serving bowl

Large pot, to cook the pasta

Wooden spoon, to stir the pasta

Colander, to drain the pasta

INGREDIENTS

1⅓ pounds kale, stemmed

5 tablespoons extra-virgin olive oil, divided

1 garlic clove, crushed

1½ cups chopped flat-leaf parsley

3 anchovies

Sea salt

6 ounces Gorgonzola, roughly chopped

Finely grated Pecorino Romano, to serve (optional)

1. Cook the kale in a pot of salted boiling water until tender, about 5 minutes. When ready, remove with a slotted spoon and reserve the cooking liquid. Roughly chop the kale.

2. Heat 2 tablespoons of oil in a saucepan over medium-low heat. Add the garlic and sauté for 2 minutes. Add the cooked kale along with ¼ cup of the reserved cooking liquid, and mix well. Season with sea salt.

3. To prepare the green sauce, combine the parsley, anchovies, and the remaining 3 tablespoons of oil in a food processor, and process until smooth. Add a tablespoon of water if necessary to make the sauce smooth.

4. Cook the pasta of your choice in the reserved kale cooking water. When the pasta is cooked, drain it and put it back into the pot over low heat.

5. Add the kale sauce and mix well while cooking on low for 1 minute.

6. Transfer to a big serving bowl, add the green sauce and Gorgonzola, and mix.

7. Serve immediately with finely grated Pecorino Romano on the top (optional).

GREAT WITH: Orecchiette (page 72) and Strascinati (page 60).

TIP: For this recipe, you can use either Gorgonzola *dolce* (which is creamier and milder) or Gorgonzola *piccante* (which is crumbly and sharp).

spicy pork ragù

There are two kinds of Italian ragù: One is made using ground meat, typical of Northern Italy, and the other is made using chunks of meat and is more common in the south. This recipe falls under the latter category. I learned how to make this sauce from my paternal grandmother, Maria, who used to make the best pork ragù I have ever eaten. In fact, I liked it so much that she would always make sure to prepare this sauce whenever I visited her in Palermo. If you like spicy food and bold flavors, this sauce is an absolute treat for the taste buds. This is comfort food at its best, and I highly recommend it for a family Sunday supper. **SERVES 4**

PREP TIME: 15 MINUTES | **COOK TIME:** 2 HOURS

EQUIPMENT

Big serving bowl

Large pot, to cook the sauce

Large pot, to cook the pasta

Wooden spoon, to stir the pasta

Colander, to drain the pasta

INGREDIENTS

3 tablespoons extra-virgin olive oil

1 onion, chopped

2 garlic cloves, chopped

1 teaspoon red pepper flakes

1 (2½-inch) piece Pecorino Romano rind with the outside scrubbed or shaved off (optional)

1 pound pork belly, cut into 1½-inch pieces

1 small rack of pork ribs, cut into 4 pieces

9 ounces Italian pork sausage

¾ pound tomato paste

5 ounces tomato purée

½ teaspoon fennel seeds

Sea salt

4 to 5 cups water

6 tablespoons ricotta cheese, mashed with a fork, to serve (optional)

Finely grated Pecorino Romano, to serve

1. Heat the oil in a saucepan over medium-low heat. Add the onion, garlic, red pepper flakes, and Pecorino Romano rind (if using), and cook, stirring constantly, so the cheese doesn't stick to the bottom of the pan, for about 3 minutes. When the onion is soft, add the pork belly, pork ribs, and Italian pork sausage, and brown it well on all sides. Be careful not to break the sausage. Add the tomato paste, tomato purée, and fennel seeds. Mix well. Season with sea salt and add enough water to cover the meat.

2. Cover and cook on low for 1½ hours, or until the sauce thickens and the meat falls off the bone. Remove the pot from the heat and discard the Pecorino Romano rind.

3. If using ricotta, mix it with the sauce in a serving bowl until creamy.

4. When the pasta is cooked, drain it and mix it in the serving bowl with the sauce.

5. Serve immediately with finely grated Pecorino Romano on the top.

GREAT WITH: Spaghetti alla Chitarra (page 106), Fettuccine (page 90), Cavatelli (page 46), Mafalde (page 98), Lasagnette (page 82), Fusilli Avellinesi (page 68), Maccheroni col Ferretto (page 66), Orecchiette (page 72), Cavatelli (page 46), and Malloreddus (page 56).

TIP: You can either debone the meat and serve it together with the pasta, or serve it separately as a second course. If you can find it, use Sicilian-style pork sausage with fennel for extra flavor. In this case, don't add any extra fennel seeds.

sausage sauce

You can make sausage sauce in many different ways. In fact, I think every Italian family has its own recipe for it, and trust me, they all taste great! In the olden days, pork was much cheaper than beef, so it was more widely available to the common folk. Pork sausages were often used to make ragù instead of ground beef, especially in rural areas. This is my family's version: simple yet tasty. **SERVES 4**

PREP TIME: 10 MINUTES | **COOK TIME:** 1 HOUR

EQUIPMENT

Knife

Cutting board

Saucepan

Large pot, to cook the pasta

Wooden spoon, to stir the pasta

Colander, to drain the pasta

INGREDIENTS

3 tablespoons extra-virgin olive oil

1 onion, chopped

9 ounces Italian pork sausage

⅓ cup white wine

1 (24-ounce) can diced tomatoes or tomato puree

1 bay leaf

2 cups water

Sea salt

Freshly ground black pepper

Finely grated Parmigiano-Reggiano or Pecorino Romano, to serve

1. Heat the oil in a saucepan over medium-low heat. Add the onion and sauté for about 2 minutes or until soft. Remove the sausage from the casing, chop it, and add it to the onion. Brown well, breaking up the lumps with a wooden spoon. Add the wine and raise the heat to burn off the alcohol. Add the tomatoes, bay leaf, and water. Season with sea salt and freshly ground black pepper. Cook the sauce over low heat for 20 minutes.

2. When the pasta is cooked, drain it and mix it with the sauce.

3. Serve immediately with finely grated Pecorino Romano or Parmigiano-Reggiano on the top.

GREAT WITH: Malloreddus (page 56), Pappardelle (page 88), Mafalde (page 98), Lasagnette (page 82), Spaghetti alla Chitarra (page 106), Maltagliati (page 80), Stringozzi (page 104), and Lagane (page 86).

TIP: If you prefer a hint of sweetness in your sauce, add 1 carrot, chopped, when sautéing the onion and use brandy or Marsala wine instead of white wine. In this case, I recommend Parmigiano-Reggiano as the cheese of choice.

ragù alla bolognese

Ragù alla Bolognese is one of the most renowned pasta sauces outside of Italy, and for a good reason: It tastes amazing. I learned how to make this recipe from my grandmother Bice. It was one of her best specialties. As a child, I remember eagerly waiting for the sauce to cook on the stove so that I could enjoy Nonna's special pasta. Her secret? She would add lots of carrots to her version, and that would give the sauce a sweeter taste that balanced out the acidity of the tomatoes. **SERVES 4**

PREP TIME: 10 MINUTES | **COOK TIME:** 1 HOUR

EQUIPMENT

Saucepan

Large pot, to cook the pasta

Wooden spoon, to stir the pasta

Colander, to drain the pasta

INGREDIENTS

3 tablespoons extra-virgin olive oil

1 onion, finely chopped

1 celery stalk, finely chopped

1 carrot, finely chopped

1 pound ground beef

⅓ cup red wine

1 (28-ounce) can diced tomatoes

4 cups water

Sea salt

Freshly ground black pepper

1 tablespoon chopped flat-leaf parsley

Finely grated Parmigiano-Reggiano, to serve

1. Heat the oil in a saucepan over medium-low heat. Add the onion, celery, and carrot, and sauté for about 5 minutes, or until soft. Stir often and make sure not to burn the vegetables. Add the ground beef and stir well with a wooden spoon, breaking up all the lumps, until the meat is browned, about 5 minutes. Add the red wine and raise the heat to burn off the alcohol. Add the tomatoes and water. Mix and season with sea salt and freshly ground black pepper.

2. Cover and cook over low heat for about 1 hour, stirring occasionally. Add the chopped parsley and remove the pan from the heat.

3. When the pasta is cooked, drain it and mix it with the sauce.

4. Serve immediately with finely grated Parmigiano-Reggiano on the top.

GREAT WITH: Tagliatelle (page 92), Fettuccine (page 90), Strozzapreti (page 64), Pici (page 54), Lagane (page 86), Potato Gnocchi (page 152), Tortellini Bolognesi (page 140), and Cappelletti Romagnoli (page 134).

TIP: If the sauce dries up too much, add a little water; if it's too runny, reduce it by cooking it on the stove. The sauce shouldn't be too thick—rather, it will be a bit more watery than a typical pasta sauce.

GLOSSARY

'zdora: A woman from Emilia-Romagna who specializes at rolling pasta dough by hand.

aglio: Garlic.

al dente: Pasta cooked to be firm to the bite.

arrabbiato/a: Angry.

Bergamasco/a: From the city of Bergamo.

Bolognese/i: From the city of Bologna.

buso: Wooden stick from a plant that grows in abundance in Sicily.

cappelletto/i: Little hat/s.

chitarra: Guitar.

crudo: Raw.

cuore/i: Heart/s.

di magro: Meatless.

durum wheat: A very hard, yellow colored wheat, with a high gluten content.

fagottino/a: Little parcel.

ferretto: A special metal skewer used to make hollow and straight cylinder pasta shapes.

fettuccia: Little slice.

fuso: Spindle.

Genovese: From the city of Genoa.

gluten: A mixture of two proteins present in cereal grains, especially wheat, which is responsible for the elastic texture of dough.

Gorgonzola: Italian mild blue cheese.

Italian speck: Italian smoked prosciutto from South Tyrol.

malloreddu: The Sardinian term for "baby calf."

mascarpone: A soft, mild Italian cream cheese.

nonna: Grandmother.

Ogliastrino/a: From Ogliastra, an area in Eastern Sardinia.

pappare: To gobble up.

Parmigiano-Reggiano: Hard Italian cheese made from cow's milk in the Emilia-Romagna region.

Pecorino Romano: Hard Italian cheese made from sheep's milk very common in the center and South of Italy.

pesto: A sauce of crushed ingredients.

quadrato/i: Square/s.

rasula: A small metal dough scraper with a long handle used to make strascinati.

ricotta: A soft, fresh, and unsalted Italian cheese.

ricotta salata: A pressed, salted, dried, and aged variety of ricotta cheese, often used grated.

Romagnolo/i: From Romagna.

stringhe: Shoelaces.

stella/e: Star/s.

tagliare: To cut.

tondo/i: Round/s.

Trapanese: From the city of Trapani.

trattoria/e: An Italian eatery, less formal than a restaurant and with casual service.

RESOURCES

VIDEO TUTORIALS

Pasta and Gnocchi Tutorials on Manu's Menu

http://www.manusmenu.com/tips/techniques
/pasta-and-gnocchi

Manu's Menu YouTube Channel

https://www.youtube.com/channel
/UCYRMY_-mXRrwdIYMiPMy9RA

**YouTube video of hand-shaped pasta
from Apulia**

https://www.youtube.com/watch?v=Hx_kPh-9J-g

Egg Pasta

https://www.youtube.com/watch?v=6hhnTGlx2DM

Durum Wheat Pasta

https://www.youtube.com/watch?v=-Vd96yFDmgM

Strozzapreti

https://www.youtube.com/watch?v=T_vSJdl-jqc

Spaghetti alla Chitarra

https://www.youtube.com/watch?v=FJo3cxD0AuY

Garganelli

https://www.youtube.com/watch?v=yW2MLbAFSZs

Culurgiones

https://www.youtube.com/watch?v=3Pyoz3GDgaE

Cappelletti

https://www.youtube.com/watch?v=QhsdTpgn7xI

Tortellini

https://www.youtube.com/watch?v=WM5M3y1EJzo

Casoncelli

https://www.youtube.com/watch?v=PqwcdfUvTgc

MEASUREMENT CONVERSIONS

VOLUME EQUIVALENTS (LIQUID)

US STANDARD	US STANDARD (OUNCES)	METRIC (APPROXIMATE)
2 tablespoons	1 fl. oz.	30 mL
¼ cup	2 fl. oz.	60 mL
½ cup	4 fl. oz.	120 mL
1 cup	8 fl. oz.	240 mL
1½ cups	12 fl. oz.	355 mL
2 cups or 1 pint	16 fl. oz.	475 mL
4 cups or 1 quart	32 fl. oz.	1 L
1 gallon	128 fl. oz.	4 L

OVEN TEMPERATURES

FAHRENHEIT (F)	CELSIUS (C) (APPROXIMATE)
250°F	120°C
300°F	150°C
325°F	165°C
350°F	180°C
375°F	190°C
400°F	200°C
425°F	220°C
450°F	230°C

VOLUME EQUIVALENTS (DRY)

US STANDARD	METRIC (APPROXIMATE)
⅛ teaspoon	0.5 mL
¼ teaspoon	1 mL
½ teaspoon	2 mL
¾ teaspoon	4 mL
1 teaspoon	5 mL
1 tablespoon	15 mL
¼ cup	59 mL
⅓ cup	79 mL
½ cup	118 mL
⅔ cup	156 mL
¾ cup	177 mL
1 cup	235 mL
2 cups or 1 pint	475 mL
3 cups	700 mL
4 cups or 1 quart	1 L

WEIGHT EQUIVALENTS

US STANDARD	METRIC (APPROXIMATE)
½ ounce	15 g
1 ounce	30 g
2 ounces	60 g
4 ounces	115 g
8 ounces	225 g
12 ounces	340 g
16 ounces or 1 pound	455 g

RECIPE INDEX

223

INDEX

ACKNOWLEDGMENTS

This book would not have been possible without my husband, Clint. Thank you for supporting me during this project and in everything I do. You are my rock!

Thanks to my daughters, Victoria and Georgia, for their love, patience, and understanding when mommy was too busy to play or help out with homework.

Thanks to my parents, Pier Giorgio and Laura, for helping out with the kids and for instilling in me the love for cooking . . . and eating. You will always be my inspiration.

Thanks to my grandparents, and especially my grandmothers, Nonna Bice and Nonna Maria, for teaching me the art of home cooking and some of the recipes in this book.

Thanks to my editor, Andrew Yackira, for his infinite patience and to all the team at Callisto Media for giving me this fantastic opportunity. You all are amazing!

ABOUT THE AUTHOR

Manuela Zangara is an Italian native who currently resides in Australia. She is the author of Manu's Menu, a food blog about traditional Italian cuisine that she started in 2011. She is also a freelance food writer and photographer, developing recipes for online magazines and brands.

She comes from a family that loves and has a strong connection with food, so her recipes and helpful tips in the kitchen have been well tested. Born and brought up in Milan to Sicilian parents, she has a passion for regional Italian food and produce. Manuela strongly believes that using the best possible ingredients in a simple way is the key to traditional, authentic, and delicious Italian food.

She has authored various eBooks on Italian food and recipes, the most recent of which—*The Cool Side of Summer*—on frozen treats, was published in 2015. You can find her on Facebook, Instagram, and Pinterest: @manusmenu.

CPSIA information can be obtained
at www.ICGtesting.com
Printed in the USA
LVHW011501280819
629035LV00003B/5/P

9 781623 159184